IMMUNITY-BUILDING SMOOTHIE BOWLS,
GREEN DRINKS, ENERGY BARS, AND MORE!

superfood boost

ERICA PALMCRANTZ AZIZ

PHOTOGRAPHY BY BIANCA BRANDON-COX

TRANSLATED BY GUN PENHOAT

Skyhorse Publishing

Original Swedish version:
Text by Erica Palmcrantz Aziz
Photography by Bianca Brandon-Cox
Graphic Design by Kai Ristilä
Styling by Bianca Brandon-Cox and Erica Palmcrantz Aziz
Edited by Åsa Karsberg

The information contained in this book is based on the author's experience and research. Consult with a physician or healthcare professional concerning questions about your health, nutrition, and medical needs.

Skyhorse Publishing books may be purchased in bulk at special discounts for sales promotion, corporate gifts, fund-raising, or educational purposes. Special editions can also be created to specifications. For details, contact the Special Sales Department, Skyhorse Publishing, 307 West 36th Street, 11th Floor, New York, NY 10018 or info@skyhorsepublishing.com.

Skyhorse® and Skyhorse Publishing® are registered trademarks of Skyhorse Publishing, Inc.®, a Delaware corporation.

Visit our website at www.skyhorsepublishing.com.

10 9 8 7 6 5 4 3 2 1

Library of Congress Cataloging-in-Publication Data

Names: Palmcrantz Aziz, Erica, 1977- author.
Title: Superfood boost: immunity-building smoothie bowls, green drinks,
    energy bars, and more / Erica Palmcrantz Aziz ; photography by Bianca
    Brandon-Cox; translated by Gun Penhoat.
Other titles: Superfood boost. English
Description: New York, New York: Skyhorse Publishing, 2018. | Translation
    from the original Swedish version published under the same title:
    Superfood boost. | Includes index. |
Identifiers: LCCN 2017044376 (print) | LCCN 2017046369 (ebook) | ISBN
    9781510731608 (E-book) | ISBN 9781510731592 (hardcover: alk. paper) |
    ISBN 9781510731608 (eBook)
Subjects: LCSH: Functional foods. | Cooking (Natural foods) | Health. |
    LCGFT: Cookbooks.
Classification: LCC QP144.F85 (ebook) | LCC QP144.F85 P3513 2018 (print) |
    DDC 613.2—dc23
LC record available at https://lccn.loc.gov/2017044376

ISBN: 978-1-5107-3159-2
eBook ISBN: 978-1-5107-3160-8

Printed in China

CONTENTS

FOREWORD
my journey

Twelve years ago, I fell in love with raw foods. It happened when I stepped into my cousin's kitchen in California and came face to face with 88 pounds (40 kg) of oranges, as well as sun-ripened tomatoes and freshly picked avocados, on the kitchen counter. I hardly knew what raw food was or what it meant. Could one really live on only fruit, vegetables, nuts, and seeds?

The answer came pretty quickly: yes, it is possible. And not only can you live on the stuff, it is pure superfood—a true health boost. It's food as medicine, coming straight from nature.

My own health surged. I thought I was feeling pretty good overall, but I got to experience what it feels like to be truly well. Gone were the blood-sugar blues, the water retention, and the noisy, gas-filled gut. And it wasn't only my physiological well-being that improved—my entire being felt so much happier!

I was off to a fantastic start thanks to all the support I got from my cousin and her family, who had adopted this healthy lifestyle to the fullest. It felt like an adventure to pick up fresh oranges from the local grower, to shop for fresh and organic produce at the Farmers Market, and to discover the wild foodstuffs that could be found in nature.

After spending ten weeks with my cousin and her family, raw food had captured my body and heart. Back in Sweden, I began trying the lifestyle on my own, and started writing Sweden's first raw food recipe book.

I still find this food just as fun and tasty now as before. A lot has happened on the raw food scene in Sweden since I got into it, and it has been great to be able to follow its progress. I'm truly dedicated to getting people to live healthier lives, and with this book my aim is to inspire you to invite superfoods and raw food into your life. I'd like to show you that it doesn't have to be especially complicated or time-consuming to live more healthily. So why not start with a snack?

See you in the health-food aisle at the grocery store!

Hugs,
Erica

INTRODUCTION

let's get to it!

These days there's a lot of talk about food's impact on our health as well as on our environment; perhaps you're one of those individuals who strives to live a little healthier and who would like to have a bit more energy every day. But how do you do it? Where do you start? The answer is simple. To see an improvement in health, more wholesome food needs to sneak into day-to-day living. It is the small, daily choices that make the greatest impact.

With this book, I want to show you that it is neither difficult nor time-consuming to eat healthy. Here you'll find recipes that are so simple that you can get them ready in only five or ten minutes. A few of them call for some drying in the oven, which will, of course, require a bit more time, but you can prepare a larger batch, which will last you longer. And you don't have to go *all out*—you're already taking a big step towards having more energy and a better quality of life if you swap a snack or two for some of the recipes in the book!

Food with superpowers are dear to my heart, and it is with great pleasure that I share with you how you can enhance your health with fresh raw ingredients, powerful seeds, interesting powders, and other revitalizing ingredients. These are simple, quick snacks made of superfoods that will boost your health. Whether you're just starting to touch lightly on what superfoods entail, or you are already adept at raw food, I hope to be able to inspire you and help you along the way.

In the first section of the book I'll go over 25 superfoods, and suggest how you can create new routines. You'll also be introduced to the raw food pyramid, and learn more about its different categories. Next you'll find delicious recipes that are guaranteed to help you start a healthier life. Once you feel confident with these recipes, I hope you will use them as the starting point for your own creations and combinations.

When I began my own raw food journey, it was with easy recipes that, once mastered, spurred me on in my own creativity. I've kept these recipes with me through the years, and they 'rescue' my everyday foods. I save my more intricate recipes and delicious desserts for the weekend or for holidays. My food needs to be fast to prepare, because I make different meals for my family and for myself; the recipes I've gathered in this book often save the day. Maybe they can become part of your diet, and can help you boost your health?

*It's simple—no complicated ingredients
or specialty tools are necessary!*

SUPERFOODS
food with superpowers

WHAT ARE SUPERFOODS?

In a nutshell, superfoods are exactly what the word says they are: raw ingredients that have superpowers. They might be leafy greens, fruits, and berries, but also nuts, seeds, oils, powders, or spices, and herbs. If you combine the various superpower ingredients that I talk about in this book, you'll get all the necessary amino acids, healthy fats, slow-release carbohydrates, fiber, chlorophyll, antioxidants, and minerals that you need.

Every fruit and vegetable has its own specific nutritional composition; in this book, I highlight a few ingredients that stand out a little more from the rest due to their nutritional value, those which can provide you with both extra health benefits and superpowers. The colors, the scents, the nutrients, and the many different shapes—isn't it amazing what nature has managed to create!

WHERE CAN YOU FIND THEM?

Many superfoods hide in plain sight in the fruit and vegetable aisle of your regular supermarket. Imagine if every raw ingredient had a label highlighting their specific benefit to your health—that would be so great!

For the most part, there are lots of superfoods at the grocery store. Where you find them differs from store to store, but it's becoming more common now for shops to dedicate, and even to create, a special health section or one devoted to whole, raw foods. Quality varies widely among grocers, so you have to try them out. Go for organic produce as often as you can. What you can't find at your local supermarket, you're likely to find in a health food store or online. Today, much is just a mouse-click away. This is very convenient if you live in a smaller community where choice is limited.

I presume you're aware that you do have influence over what is available at your local grocery store; if you let the produce managers know what is missing from their selection, they'll probably be happy to help and order it for you.

QUICK SNACKS

Superfoods make perfect nutrient-rich snacks. We seldom plan our nibbling, so we often end up eating an apple on the go, a chocolate chip cookie in the afternoon, a few pieces of candy when we're shopping for dinner, or a cinnamon bun during our coffee break. It might be due to snacking that our energy levels remain steady and elevated throughout the day, so naturally it's important that we choose the *right* type of snack. It's both easy and healthy to load the refrigerator and freezer with chia puddings, smoothies, balls, and wholesome raw food ice creams.

The recipes included in *Superfood Boost* work equally well for breakfast, lunch, or dinner—whenever you want to eat something light but still full of energy.

Superfood Boost is the new black! Energizing yourself with superfoods will keep you right on track and on trend.

HEALTH

inner and outer wellness

HAVE MORE ENERGY, BE HAPPIER, AND BE HEALTHIER WITH THE RIGHT RAW INGREDIENTS

It may sound clichéd that you can become all of the following—alert, energetic, happy, and attractive—by eating food that contains important nutrients. But by letting in raw foods with health boosting properties, you'll just feel so much better.

What we eat imbues us with the energy we need. However, if you feed your body empty calories, it's only a momentary stopgap. The body and the brain require a combination of essential fats, amino acids, minerals, and vitamins to function optimally. By giving your body superfoods, there are no empty calories and you don't burden your body with foods that are hard to convert into energy. By eating regular snacks, you'll also keep your energy level stable and avoid surges and crashes. Superfoods refill your energy account so you can get just a little bit more done.

Superfoods are also rich in antioxidants, which protect against illness. Picture your immune system as a protective, armored shield—you'll want that shield to be as solid as possible. If you don't get enough antioxidants, your armor will rust and develop holes where bacteria and viruses can easily work their way in.

The link between the health of your gut and how happy you are has proven to be very strong. Superfoods contribute beneficial bacteria to your gut flora, as well as fiber, which keeps your digestive system in good working order. A happy gut makes for a happy you. Your natural skin tone also gets perked up by superfoods. We're not talking about what size clothes you wear, what your nose looks like, or the color of your hair—here, beauty truly radiates from the inside. However, if you wish to lose extra weight, get a glowing complexion, and sparkling eyes, superfoods will see to all of that.

YOUR OPTIMAL HEALTH

Health is about much more than just food. It is about how we sleep, whether we're active or not, our relationships, our work situation—our entire lifestyle influences our health. Life is based on energy. You can raise your energy by inviting in food that has retained its nutrients and its life-giving enzymes. Don't fool yourself with coffee and sugar—that's only borrowed energy.

It's that small detail that can be crucial to your health. If you omit something that is unhealthy every day and choose something that is good for you instead—that's when your actions have an impact. And you're going to notice it in the way you feel!

At times when I am not mindful about what I eat, I soon feel that I don't have the same level of energy, joy, and lightness in my body. And when I take the car instead of my bicycle to go somewhere, I can tell the difference immediately! Start off with small changes and feel the difference. That way you'll become motivated to do more, which in turn will make you feel even better.

Do you already feel on top of the world, and don't have any aches and pains? It's still worth your while to give it a try. Test the recipes and include a few more superfoods and raw foods into your diet, and see how they make you feel. Before I started with raw foods, I thought my baseline condition was good. However, it wasn't until now that I fully realize what feeling good feels like.

You've heard all this before:
- *Take the stairs, not the elevator*
- *Walk to a stop further away*
- *Bike instead of taking the car*
- *Drink a green smoothie every day*

Thirty minutes a day of activity that raises your heart rate is generally recommended. It's not about working yourself into a frazzle and sweating copiously—no, it's about daily exercise. But make sure that your workout doesn't become an excuse for indulging in unhealthy eating, as in "I have exercised, therefore I deserve a treat." Those calories might be used up and your body may be better at handling the flood of insulin generated by sweets, but why pull apart what you've tried to build up? Keep an eye on small details that can have such an impact on the overall picture!

Spending money on food that ruins your health—and then taking medicine and supplements to get well again and to rebuild your health—that's just a waste of cash. Start by strengthening your body with natural and complete nutrition; that is the way to truly invest in yourself. Scrap the costly 'middleman,' i.e., illness and lethargy.

When you're ill you only want to get better; but when you're healthy, you can wish for thousands of other things!

Unhealthy food, stress, and not enough exercise and sleep can be compared to a credit card: we borrow and borrow, but one day the bill comes due. Unfortunately, it can be expensive to pay back the borrowed energy that we've used up. Using food as preventive measure for good health is vital.

- *Choose health*
- *Choose proper nutrition, and eat to achieve balance*
- *Investing in your health is worth every penny*

FIND YOUR WEIGHT

We have never been so overweight in the Western world—as well as so malnourished—as we are today. We eat until we're full, yet our body still clamors for nutrients. So we give it more nutrient-poor food, again. This food robs us of energy, nibbles away at our reserves, and causes us to put on weight. Our body is idling, and sooner or later illness can come sneaking in.

The body requires the right type of fuel. It needs a certain amount of calories, but calories that are loaded with nutrition. If we feed it the opposite—empty calories without nutrients—we can't achieve long-term weight loss and improve our health. By making better food choices daily and adding superfoods to our diet, weight can be stabilized without unnecessary hunger pangs or mood swings. Say no to empty calories!

INNER HEALTH = OUTER HEALTH

Both our inner and outer health are affected by what we eat—we can't eat junk food and expect it to not show on the outside. Superfoods not only boost our inner health, we also notice our body's improved condition in our complexion, hair, nails, and weight. Food that is full of nutrients makes us feel great inside and out!

8 reason why you should start boosting with superfoods

To be more energetic and have more vitality.

To lose weight and have a slimmer body.

To become happier and be more positive.

To keep yourself more healthy.

To feel stronger and more alert.

To feel calmer and less stressed.

To sleep better.

To clear brain fog.

VEGETABLE BASED

Research shows that we all feel better if we consume lots of fruit, leafy greens, and other vegetable-based food, and that vegans and vegetarians are in better overall health throughout life. Eating a vegetable-based diet reduces the risk for cardio-vascular disease, diabetes, cataracts, and arthritis, and contributes to healthy weight reduction. Our lifestyle and our own individual metabolism affects what we choose to eat (per our personal ethics) or what makes us feel good.

Why not try eating less meat and more vegetables for a month or two and see if it makes you feel better? Research is all fine and good, but it's easier to understand its effects on health if you try for yourself.

GOOD FOR THE PLANET

We are more and more aware of how our food choices affect our bodies, our minds, as well as our planet. It has become second nature for many of us to seek out organic produce. It's impossible to close our eyes to the fact that the choices we make for our own health also affect the health of our planet. This may make things cost a little bit more, and occasionally way more—but I really recommend that you make organic food your first choice as often as you can afford to. Organic produce has shown to be more nutrient-dense, and it is of course better to eat raw foods that are not laden with chemicals. Another rule of thumb is to try and buy seasonal products. They taste better and are a climate-friendlier option.

The world's consumption of meat also poses one of the greatest threats to our environment, so there is a lot to be gained from reducing the amount of meat we eat and increasing our vegetable intake, for both our health and the environment. There is an old saying that goes that you should always think seven generations ahead when making a decision; maybe there's something in that, after all.

*Raw food is a lifestyle more
than just a way of eating—
it is a conscious choice not only
for our own benefit, but also
for that of our fellow human
beings and of our planet.*

RAW FOOD
optimal nutrition

WHAT IS RAW FOOD?

A simple definition is that raw food is food that has not been heated above 107°F (42°C). That means that you'll benefit from food at its nutritional best since all the enzymes, vitamins, minerals, and nutrients remain unadulterated. The food consists of vegetables, fruit, dried fruit, root vegetables, berries, algae, beans, lentils, seeds, nuts, some grains, cold-pressed oils, raw honey, fermented vegetables, herbs, wheatgrass, and superfood powders. All the recipes in this book are made up not only of superfoods, they're also raw, which make them extra healthy.

It's common to soak nuts, seeds, and dried fruit, and also to sprout seeds, when following a raw diet. Soaking and sprouting make the food more nutritious and easier to digest. A dormant enzyme awakens and the seed comes to life when you soak nuts and seeds. The seed is easier to absorb, its nutrition is optimized, and its life force increases. Read more about how to sprout on page 31.

A FOOD PYRAMID FOR THE NEW MILLENIUM

You may already have seen the traditional food pyramid, and perhaps also its vegetable-based counterpart. In this book I have chosen to show you what the raw food pyramid looks like. The pyramid's products are vegan and are comprised of what we refer to as clean raw ingredients, i.e., ingredients that are minimally processed. The less a raw ingredient is processed, the better it is for us. That the raw ingredient has not been heated above 107°F (42°C) means that its nutrients are even more protected. Really, all raw foods can be put on a pedestal and called superfoods, because they're all made up of unique combinations of nutrients. However, in this book I've selected 25 raw ingredients that are extra nutritious and can work real wonders for your health. I encourage you to study each raw ingredient's effects further and how they influence our health. I never cease to be amazed at nature's ingenuity.

A FOOD PYRAMID FOR THE NEW MILLENIUM

Here you'll get to know all the raw food pyramid's categories.
Plan your plate using the pyramid as your guide—lots of leafy greens,
vegetables, fruits, and berries topped with algae and sprouts.
Keep chocolate and sweets to an occasional treat.

POWDERS

SWEETENERS

SEEDS/NUTS

GRAINS AND CEREALS

OILS

BERRIES

FRUIT

VEGETABLES/
ROOT VEGETABLES

LEAFY
GREENS

LEAFY GREENS

The foundation of the raw food diet is different types of leafy greens. Green is great—for both body and soul. The green color comes from chlorophyll, which is said to have a cleansing effect on our blood. Chlorophyll and our blood also show surprising similarities in their chemical structure—except that in blood you'll find iron, and in chlorophyll there's magnesium. Nowadays, many people suffer from magnesium deficiency because most of us have a very busy daily schedule. In fact, stress and tough workouts can leach magnesium from our body. Alternate between different available leafy greens, and venture out also into the nearest park or woods and forage for seasonal wild greens. What we typically call weeds—dandelions, nettles, ground elder (Bishop's weed), field horsetail—do wonders for your health. You can make it even easier and supplement your intake of green chlorophyll by adding in green powders such as nettle powder, wheatgrass powder, spirulina, and chlorella, for example.

Sprouts and shoots belong to the leafy greens category, too; read more about leafy greens on page 28.

VEGETABLES AND ROOT VEGETABLES

There are vegetables in all colors of the rainbow, and the colors indicate that there are plenty of antioxidants and other important, health-promoting nutrients in the vegetables. Cucumber and avocado are fruits, really, but we typically include them with the vegetables. See more on page 32.

Don't forget to use the leafy tops of root vegetables. The tops belong to the leafy greens category, and they're great in juices and smoothies.

The red beet is a wonderful root vegetable known mostly for its cleansing effect on the liver; more recently it has also come to be appreciated for its help in increasing oxygen uptake in connection with physical training. However, in this book I've chosen to emphasize raw foods that can be treated quickly and simply, and unfortunately the beet's delightful red color makes it impractical to use as often as I'd like. Somehow, I seem to end up with red stains everywhere. (When you peel and cut a beet, why not rub some of the pigment into your cheeks to get some of the most natural blush you could ask for!)

Read more about carrots on page 32.

FRUIT

For those of us who live in Nordic countries, it may feel very exotic to travel abroad and feast on mango and papaya, grapes and watermelon. But it's just as foreign for tourists visiting our country to see red apples, purple plums, and pears weighing down the trees here in Sweden. Swedish homegrown fruits sizzle with vitality and nutrition, but you have to hurry to pick them to make jam, juice, or dried fruit before they molder away. Try to gather and use our Swedish fruits as often as you can.

We eat imported fruit over long stretches of the year here in the north. But their level of nutrients is optimal only when the fruit is perfectly ripe, not when it has been harvested early to ripen while in transit and at the grocery store. That's why I've singled out an exotic fruit—the mango—because you can find it fresh, frozen, or dried at the supermarket. Dried mango is my personal favorite, really, because it's environmentally friendly. It's harvested and dried at the peak of freshness. It's perfect to soak dried mango a little—this makes them ideal to use in different recipes. Read more about dried, frozen, and fresh mango on page 34.

Pomegranate is another exotic fruit, but it also grows in Europe. It might be a bit awkward to open up, but you can find both frozen pomegranate and pomegranate juice if you'd rather avoid a lot of work. However, fresh pomegranate is best, and if you're going to open one you may as well go for broke and do two, and store the one you're not using immediately in the refrigerator for a few days.

BERRIES

Berries are generally loaded with nutrients and contain tons of antioxidants. We should call them "wonder berries," since they work wonders for everyone's health. You can buy most berries frozen or dried year-round, when the season for fresh berries is over. Blueberries, goji berries, cranberries, and cherries—read more about them on page 37.

GRAINS AND CEREALS

Cereals, along with potatoes, have been survival foods in Sweden. Cereal consumption has dropped due its GI (glycemic index) value, and while gluten can be a real health bad guy, not all grains are villains. Read more about buckwheat and oats on pages 38 and 39.

SEEDS AND NUTS

Pumpkin seeds, sunflower seeds, walnuts, hazelnuts (filberts)—research has shown that seeds and nuts are good for you. They contribute to cardiovascular health, balance out blood sugar, and provide fiber, essential fats, and nutrients. Tweak the recipes by using a variety of nuts and seeds to experience different flavors, textures, and nutritional combos. Read more about hemp hearts, chia seeds, and almonds on page 40.

OILS

The best oils are extracted during their first press, and through cold pressing. These are called extra virgin oil. Oil is an excellent flavoring agent, and also helps us absorb the fat-soluble vitamins in our food. You could say that fat-soluble vitamins need oil as their transporter. It's not advisable to heat a fine oil because it might be heat sensitive. Coconut oil, however, can be used at high temperatures with no ill effect.

For a change, try using oil in a bath with some added aromatic essential oils, or massage the oil directly into your skin.

There are many good oils out there, such as olive oil, almond oil, pumpkin seed oil, hemp oil, and avocado oil. Read more about coconut oil on page 42.

SWEETENERS

A smidgen of sweetener completes the flavor palette. There are several options to choose from if you're vegan and don't use honey; the recipes remain simple to follow and are just as nutritious. If you're a vegetarian or a 'beegan' (i.e., a vegan who eats honey), you can follow the recipes as written, or if you're curious, you can give one of the other alternatives a try: yacon syrup, maple syrup, or agave syrup, dried fruit, or fresh dates.

Be aware that textures may vary and that you may have to adjust the amount of sweetener from one recipe to the next, depending on which sweetener you're using.

SUPER-POWDERS

It might be a bit strange at first to think of powders as food, but I promise that once you've started to get to know and experiment with different super-powders, you'll be a convert. It's fun to play with different flavors and colors. What's so magical about powders is that they typically contain a very broad nutritional profile. You're actually getting optimal nutrition with each calorie ingested—and each dollar spent. Read more about maca and raw cacao powder on page 45.

FERMENTED FOOD

Sauerkraut is a real superfood, and there has probably never been so much talk about sauerkraut and gut flora as there is nowadays. By consuming sauerkraut on a daily basis, you're promoting good gut flora, which in turn boosts your overall health. The fact that digestive health and gut health are closely linked to the rest of our wellbeing is now widely accepted.

ALGAE

Another super-wonder-food that is not a common ingredient in the Swedish daily diet is algae. You can use algae powders such as spirulina and chlorella (they're also available in tablets) if you want to keep things simple. Nori, dulse, and arame are algae that aren't quite so algae-like, so you can sneak them in a little everywhere. You'll find kelp noodles in your grocery store's Asian food section; the noodles are deliciously crispy and free of carbohydrates, but loaded with iodine.

SPICES AND HERBS

Spices and dried and fresh herbs enhance both the flavor and the nutritional value of what you eat. And they're not only delicious—each spice and herb has its unique effect on the body. Turmeric and ginger are super roots that also impart great flavor to the dishes you make. They are best when used fresh, but they work perfectly well when dried, too. Both ginger and turmeric are true immune system super-boosters.

BEVERAGES

It has become extremely popular to use a variety of beverages with additives to boost your health. But take extra care when you read the ingredients list—what percentage is really just pure water? It could turn out to be very expensive water. It's incredibly simple to make your own super-water with herbs, berries, and powders. It's not only cool to make it yourself, you'll also control its contents so you don't have to worry that the water has weird preservatives or artificial sweeteners in it. You can read about how to make cold-brewed green tea on page 91, and on page 86 you'll learn how to prepare your own perfect matcha latte.

There are plenty of super-powders to try once you begin feeling comfortable using them. Scour your health-food store and look for:

Mesquite powder

Lucuma powder

Carob powder

Baobab powder

Camu camu powder

Acai powder

Mucuna powder

Sacha Inchi powder

Chaga mushroom powder

Reishi mushroom powder

HABITS & THE PANTRY
stock up on good ingredients!

INGREDIENTS TO HAVE ON HAND

Make sure to always have good quality ingredients at home and super-powders in the pantry; that way it's much easier to choose healthy options. Simply stock your basic pantry with the ingredients from the food pyramid, and supplement them with raw ingredients from the list below. You'll find most of the items at the grocery store or in the health-food store. You can also shop for many things online. Round them up with seasonal fresh fruit, berries, and vegetables.

ROUTINES AND HABITS

Routines and habits—that's often what runs our days, and how our bodies like it. We like doing the same things at regular intervals; however, this also means that it takes a Herculean effort to change a habit. We must accept that it will be a bit uncomfortable to let go of the old to make room for the new, which too, in turn, will soon become routine. Once your new habits become a regular thing, it might feel weird to go back to the 'old ways' that might not have made you feel your best.

Good to have on hand!

FOR SPROUTING
Mung beans
Green lentils
Buckwheat
Alfalfa
Whole hemp seeds (not de-hulled)
Whole wheat and rye kernels

NUTS & SEEDS
Almonds
Hazelnuts
Pecans
Cashews
Pistachios
Brazil nuts
Walnuts
Pine nuts
Sunflower seeds
Pumpkin seeds
Chia seeds
Flax seeds
Hemp hearts (de-hulled seeds)

DRIED FRUIT
Apricots
Prunes
Figs
Dates (fresh, not pitted)
Raisins (preferably not preserved
with sulfur dioxide)
Berries (goji berries, for example)

ALGAE
Wakame
Arame
Nori
Dulse

SUPER-POWDERS
Raw cacao powder/cacao nibs
Hemp powder
Rosehip powder
Spirulina powder
Maca powder
Nettle powder

SPICES
Vanilla powder
Cumin
Turmeric
Cayenne pepper
Chili pepper
Cinnamon

IN THE REFRIGERATOR
Tamari—a fermented soy sauce
Miso

MISCELLANEOUS
Salt (Celtic sea salt or grey sea salt)
Carob
Coconut
Nutritional yeast
Bee pollen
Yacon syrup/maple syrup
Honey

Transformational coaches and lifestyle coaches typically emphasize the importance of repetition. We could call it the power of repetition. Once you've drunk a green smoothie often enough, it becomes a habit, and once you've chosen to not eat sugar, or you grab a raw bar and some juice instead of a cinnamon bun and a cup of coffee, then it becomes your new normal.

I know firsthand how difficult it is to eat only what's healthy, and how easy it is to give in and think, 'this won't kill me.' That's why it's so much easier if you've set up a good habit. Then it becomes routine and it's not as difficult to say "no thanks" when someone offers you an unhealthy choice. So give it some time—soon the new habits will take root, and what is wholesome will be the norm.

PLAN MORE

You might think it sounds really boring and uninspiring to plan meals ahead of time, but it does simplify life enormously. Schedule your shopping, and set aside some time so you can make a day of prepping, for example, balls and bars. You'll be sure to resist the temptation of eating something bad for you when a craving or hunger pang hits, because there will be healthy food ready in the refrigerator and freezer.

What's so beneficial about snacks?

It's easier for the body to process several small meals than fewer, larger ones.

Your energy will be more evenly spread throughout the day.

With planned snacks, you avoid overeating.

You don't get so famished that you could eat a horse before sitting down to your main meals, which means that you won't inhale your food.

You'll eat less, but more mindfully.

An awesome tip is to plan ahead and make your breakfast—like, say, overnight oats—the evening before. There's nothing better than having your breakfast ready and waiting before you're even awake; we all know how that time of the morning always just blows by. Puddings and grains are also super easy to take with you in a small jar; that way you can eat breakfast on your way to work or once you're there.

SIMPLIFY

Do you have (as I do) many great-looking cookbooks at home? Hand on heart, I can say that most of the time I only browse through them and yearn for the beautiful and delicious dishes within, but how many of them do I actually make? The ingredients list is often long and may have items that are difficult to find, and the directions are complicated. However much I would love to cook this food, life suddenly gets in the way and blood sugar starts to nosedive—and then I have to come up with something quick and simple. I must think ahead and enjoy the more intricate recipes on weekends, holidays, or at parties, because everyday meals? Those have to happen in a flash.

My advice? KISS—Keep It Stupidly Simple.

SWITCH YOUR MEALS AROUND

The recipes in this book work just as well for breakfast, lunch, or dinner when you're seeking lighter food that's still packed with energy, something that's good for your body as well as your mood. Replacing lunch—which might be a microwaveable meal or yesterday's leftovers—with the book's superfood recipes, made with fresh ingredients and living foods, will provide you with stamina until evening. We have this notion that for something to be considered dinner, it should come to the table piping hot. It's far too easy to resort to cans and boxes when everyday suppers must be thrown together quickly, be nourishing, and then be cleared away just as rapidly. The superfood recipes are loaded with all the nutrients you need without making you feel stuffed and exhausted, leading you to spend your evening collapsed on the couch. And they are just as quick to make as the canned unhealthy food.

Try out some combinations of my recipes over one week—take a peek at my suggestions on page 104.

BASIC INGREDIENTS

25 superfoods that will make you feel better

You have probably shopped for these ingredients in the past, but here you'll get to know why you should buy them more often; you'll also become inspired on how to prepare them quickly and simply. These 25 ingredients top my list of favorites. You'll find out 5 quick facts about how each ingredient can boost your health and make you feel much better.

1. LEAFY GREENS AND EDIBLE WEEDS

For me, it's a dream to walk barefoot in the garden, pick my own leaves, and mix them into my morning smoothie. It's real energy that comes straight from nature, without me having to plant, water, or fertilize anything—I only have to harvest. And feel the energy! You can do exactly the same thing, even if you live in an urban area. Just go to the nearest park and start picking, but make sure to rinse the leaves thoroughly as soon as you get home.

Adding different types of leafy greens to your daily plate can make an enormous difference to your health. At times when picking wild leaves isn't possible, you'll find several kinds of greens at your nearest grocery store, such as arugula, spinach, romaine lettuce, and Swiss chard.

EDIBLE WEEDS
Ground elder (Bishop's Weed), common nettle, Lady's Mantle, broadleaf plantain, dandelion, and field horsetail are examples of health-boosting, wild, raw ingredients.

> **TOP 5 REASONS WHY YOU SHOULD EAT LEAFY GREENS**
> **1.** To fill up on chlorophyll, which is said to purify and detoxify the blood.
> 2. To feel more relaxed! Green leaves contain the important mineral magnesium; magnesium deficiency can lead you to feeling down in the dumps, and also brings on muscle cramps.
> **3.** You'll get all the essential amino acids; the leaves are also a source of complete protein.
> **4.** To build stronger bones! Green leaves contain Vitamin K, which reduces the risk of developing osteoporosis.
> **5.** Weeds grown in the wild contain a wide spectrum of nutrients, including a higher content of what are called biophotons.

2. KALE

Kale is not just for Christmas anymore—demand for this vegetable has increased year-round. Switch it up with some black cabbage (palm cabbage), a good substitute for kale since it has the same properties and health benefits as kale. Massage and toss the cabbage with some olive oil, salt, and lemon, or add it to a smoothie or juice, or enjoy it with a creamy dressing. The main thing is that you eat your kale!

> **TOP 5 REASONS WHY YOU SHOULD EAT KALE**
> **1.** It provides you with chlorophyll, which keeps your body alkaline.
> **2.** It is rejuvenating. It contains Vitamin C, which protects our skin from wrinkles.
> **3.** It is rich in the antioxidants Vitamin A, C, and E, which counteract inflammation.
> **4.** To keep yourself healthy! Kale has anti-bacterial properties.
> **5.** To get smarter! Research has shown that kale's high content of folate (natural folic acid) makes it easier for us to learn and retain information.

Super boost when you are older

As you age, your metabolism slows down, osteoporosis sets in, and your appetite might fade. While each gram of superfood provides nutrition, leafy greens lead the way in protecting you against osteoporosis. Fiber keeps you regular, and raw ingredients provide delicious flavors that stimulate the appetite. That the recipes are simple to follow and loaded with nutrients will make you go from simply retired to energetically retired!

3. SPROUTS

When you grow your own sprouts, you end up with organic and almost free food that is both local and homegrown. Alfalfa, green lentils, mung beans, beluga lentils, and broccoli seeds are examples of seeds, beans, and lentils that are great for sprouting.

It's a treat to cultivate sprouts at home in your own kitchen! I'm fascinated by how such a small seed can turn into a sprout—a sprout that will make me happier, sunnier, and healthier.

TOP 5 REASONS WHY YOU SHOULD EAT SPROUTS

1. Sprouts have high *enzyme* activity, which gives *life force*.
2. They contain all the essential amino acids.
3. They keep the digestive system working. Sprouts are packed with fiber.
4. They are rich in potassium, a mineral that affects both muscle and nerve function.
5. Sprouts can be seen as a catalyst in the body, because they help the body absorb nutrients.

HOW TO SPROUT

It's easy to grow your own sprouts—and they're tasty. As you go from seed stage to sprout, the nutrients and enzyme activity that helps us break down food and absorb other nutrients increases. It's also healthy for your wallet to grow sprouts at home. There are special sprouting boxes you can buy at the health food store or online. A sprouting box makes the task simple and could be a good investment if you intend to grow a lot of sprouts. This is how it's done:

1. Use about 1½ fl oz (1 dl) seeds/beans with approximately 2 cups (5 dl) water. Measure 2 tablespoons of seeds/beans per 2 cups (5 dl) water if you're sprouting smaller seeds such as alfalfa, garlic, or radish seeds.
2. Soak the seeds/beans for about 8 to 12 hours. (Smaller seeds like alfalfa only require 4 hours' soaking). Drain the water and rinse the seeds/beans thoroughly in a fine mesh sieve.
3. Place the seeds/beans in glass jar or bowl.
4. Cover the container to block out the light to the seeds/beans, but don't make it airtight. You can use a kitchen towel, for example, or place the seeds/beans in a dark cupboard.
5. Rinse the seeds/beans with lukewarm water at least once per day. Let them drain thoroughly each time.
6. When the sprouts' tails begin to emerge, they can continue to grow in daylight. This usually takes about 3 to 5 days, depending on the variety.
7. Store the sprouts in the refrigerator; they will keep for at least 5 days. Continue to rinse the sprouts once a day.

4. CARROTS

Our Swedish carrot can do a lot for your health! To me, the carrot is a daily life saver—if I have a bag of carrots in the refrigerator I can quickly throw together something to eat, or blend some freshly squeezed carrot juice with an avocado.

TOP 5 REASONS WHY YOU SHOULD EAT CARROTS

1. For sharper vision! The beta carotene improves your eyesight.
2. To look better! Carrots brings fresh tone to your skin.
3. The carrot's fibers (if you don't simply drink the juice) prevent constipation.
4. The green carrot tops have the same amazing nutritional value as leafy greens. Juice them or add them to a smoothie.
5. Carrots are bacteria and virus inhibitors.

5. CUCUMBER

Do cucumbers seem like an unnecessary expense? Because it's mostly water that you buy? Well, that's not the whole story. Cucumbers contribute much to your health and your body. In summertime you can bring a cooler full of cucumbers to the beach to avoid getting hooked on the ice cream lure.

TOP 5 REASONS WHY YOU SHOULD EAT CUCUMBERS

1. Their high water and silicone content will give you a lustrous complexion. Even your hair and nails will get a beauty shot.
2. In an afternoon slump? Eat a cucumber. It provides minerals and vitamins such as potassium, calcium, iron, zinc, and B vitamins. The nutrients and water will make you more alert.
3. Are you craving sweets? A cucumber could be the solution.
4. Cucumbers provide you with necessary fluid. They rehydrate the body with a liquid containing the perfect balance of minerals and salts.
5. They're ideal for weight loss! A cucumber contains few calories and no sugar. Enjoy them to your heart's content when you want to lose weight.

6. AVOCADO

An avocado and a cucumber along with some fruit can make an entire meal when I have one foot out the door. With avocado, you can assemble a variety of different meals very quickly: chocolate mousse, soup, a bowl, raw food ice cream . . . avocado is also the perfect baby food.

TOP 5 REASONS WHY YOU SHOULD EAT AVOCADOS

1. The good fats lubricate you from the inside and make your skin softer.
2. They cleanse you of fat-soluble poisons that collect in the body.
3. Vitamin E makes your skin tight and smooth.
4. Their electrolytes restore the body's mineral balance and give you more stamina.
5. Avocado has an alkaline effect on the body. An alkaline body is a healthier body.

Each ingredient has either an acidifying or alkaline effect on the body. To simplify, we can say that animal products, coffee and tea, processed foods, sugar, and white flour are all acidifying to the body, whereas fresh fruits and vegetables, super-powders, and seeds have an alkaline effect. We must unburden the body and help it retain its alkaline environment; we do this by eating wholesome foods.

7. MANGO

Mango is sold fresh, frozen, and dried; my favorite kind of mango is the dried variety. I like it because, when soaked, it helps add the right creaminess for smoothies, mylk-shakes, and ice cream. It's also the most environmentally friendly type of mango available at the grocery store. You can use frozen mango in the same way, but you'll need to defrost it if you don't want a frosted smoothie.

TOP 5 REASONS WHY YOU SHOULD EAT MANGOES

1. Mango is a delight for the gut! Its fibers keep you regular, and provide feelings of satiety.
2. It has good sweetening power! Mango is sweet, but it does not elevate blood sugar significantly due to its fiber content.
3. It is rich in Vitamins A, C, and E, which strengthen the immune system.
4. It maintains kidney function and helps cleanse the body.
5. Mango's level of beta carotene is good for your eyes' health.

8. POMEGRANATE

There are many seeds in pomegranates and it's a bit of a mess to get them all out. My tip is to cut the pomegranate in half and squeeze the peel until it's soft, and then turn the peel inside out. Remove any remaining white pieces of peel. You can also strike the peel with the back of a spoon, over a bowl, and the pips will come loose and fall out. Or you can opt for the easy way: buy the pomegranate frozen! Pomegranates work well both in savory dishes and sweets, and makes a delicious topping for a bowl.

TOP 5 REASON WHY YOU SHOULD EAT POMEGRANATES

1. Here you'll find more flavonoids than in green tea, cacao, and red wine. Flavonoids are antioxidants that protect the heart and blood vessels.
2. They can repair damage caused by high cholesterol.
3. They protect against dementia—one of the pomegranate's beneficial properties is that it scours the blood vessels.
4. They offer natural sun protection—their antioxidants protect your skin against the sun's rays.
5. Research has shown that the super-antioxidants present in pomegranates might have a protective effect against certain forms of cancer.

9. GOJI BERRIES

Goji berries originated in China, but these days they're grown even in Sweden. For thousands of years Chinese medicine has thought them to have rejuvenating properties. Taking one tablespoon of goji berries per day can provide the necessary amount of some nutrients we need daily to achieve optimal heath. The red color comes from the berries' high content of carotenoids, which are antioxidants.

TOP 5 REASONS WHY YOU SHOULD EAT GOJI BERRIES

1. They are rich in iron; iron deficiency can make us feel tired. Women may need extra iron, especially during their childbearing years.
2. To improve your eyesight! Goji berries are said to contain more beta carotene than carrots.
3. They are rich in magnesium and the essential nutrient thiamine, which can improve the quality of your sleep.
4. To be as healthy as a goji berry! Forget your multivitamin, and eat goji berries every day instead.
5. To stay young longer! Goji berries' high level of antioxidants will help you fight premature aging.

10. BLUEBERRIES

Blueberries are one of our Nordic superfoods that we can pick, free of charge, in all our pine forests. Since many of us do not take the time to venture out into nature to collect these blue jewels, we should be grateful that they can be found in the frozen foods aisle, or freeze-dried, or in powder form, at the grocery store. The blueberry is a fruit we can derive much benefit from by eating it several times a week.

TOP 5 REASONS WHY YOU SHOULD EAT BLUEBERRIES

1. It's good for your skin!
2. For improved circulation! Blueberries contain compounds that boost blood circulation.
3. To have fewer cravings for sweets! Blueberries stabilize blood sugar levels.
4. You'll have a happy gut! Eat blueberries together with probiotics, since they fight inflammation in the digestive tract.
5. To see better in the dark! Compounds in blueberries improve night vision.

11. CRANBERRIES

These berries are small, red, and very tart, so why on earth should we eat them? Aside from the health aspect, they impart freshness if you combine them with something sweet, and their tartness adds zip to any salad or cooked entrée. Why not make a Nordic salsa with cranberries, mango, avocado, and parsley? I make raw jam with either fresh or frozen cranberries mixed with coconut palm sugar or xylitol.

TOP 5 REASONS WHY YOU SHOULD EAT CRANBERRIES

1. Research shows that if fat and cranberries are eaten at the same meal, the body will not absorb the fat.
2. To steady blood sugar levels! Cranberries are tart, which is a sign that they won't spike blood sugar.
3. Cranberries, like grapes, contain resveratrol which, according to research, decreases the risk of developing cancer.
4. To prevent diabetes! Cranberries contain quercetin, which promotes better insulin sensitivity.
5. Cranberries contain polyphenols, which help lower cholesterol.

12. CHERRIES

If you've ever stained your clothes while eating cherries, you know that you'll never get those spots out. As irritating as it can be in the case of ruined garments, the strong color that stubbornly stays put is proof of the powerful antioxidants contained in cherries—antioxidants that strengthen the immune system and bolster your body's ability to create super health.

TOP 5 REASONS WHY YOU SHOULD EAT CHERRIES

1. For their anti-inflammatory effect! Cherries are one of the berries that are richest in antioxidants.
2. To suffer less post-workout agony! According to research, the antioxidants in cherries can actually prevent exercise pain.
3. To banish that headache! Compounds in cherries can help prevent headache and migraine.
4. To strengthen your kidneys. Cherries lower levels of uric acid in the body.
5. For suppler joints! Uric acid in the body can be detrimental to our joints. Cherries lower the levels of uric acid.

13. BUCKWHEAT

Buckwheat comes in many forms: whole and unhulled, hulled, as flakes, and as flour. It's the hulled buckwheat you should use in my recipes. Buckwheat does require a bit of preparation; in order to absorb all the health benefits from buckwheat, we need to soak it and sprout it a little. It isn't complicated—it just needs to become a new habit. There's nothing to it; it's like doing a dance: once you've become used to soaking and sprouting, your life dance will become far more efficient. Buckwheat is an herbal knot grass and is naturally gluten-free.

TOP 5 REASONS WHY YOU SHOULD EAT BUCKWHEAT

1. Buckwheat contains all the essential amino acids which are great for you when you're working out.
2. This herb contains slow-release carbohydrates, which provide steady stamina and energy throughout the day.
3. You'll be better-tempered! Your mood will even out due to the slow carbohydrates.
4. Buckwheat provides the gut with fiber to work with, without overdoing it. It lies softly, like cotton, in your stomach.
5. It protects the heart. Research shows that buckwheat protects against high cholesterol, which in turn can lower the risk of cardiovascular disease.

Gluten can irritate the lining of the stomach and lead to inflammation, which in turn can cause a leaky gut, a gassy and bloated abdomen, mood swings, and achy joints.

14. OATS

You can buy oats as flakes or as groats. Naked oats, an older version of oats, have a higher nutrient density than regular oats. The healthiest way to use them is to soak the whole groats overnight and then sprout them for a few days; that way you keep the 'rawness' in the oats. Add them to salads and chia puddings, or mix them into a smoothie.

Oat flakes or oat grains are rolled and flattened oat groats, and the kernels may have been heated in the process. There is a 'raw' grain that has been cold-rolled instead of steam processed, allowing all nutrients to be preserved. By all means, try out the cold-processed oats if you can find them.

Heads up! Soak grains that are going to be eaten raw to remove what are called enzyme inhibitors, which can prevent the body from absorbing calcium, magnesium, iron, and zinc.

TOP 5 REASONS WHY YOU SHOULD EAT OATS
1. The Vitamin E in oats kills inflammation in the body.
2. Raw oats make you fill full for longer.
3. Vitamin E, which is a natural antioxidant, fights free radicals, and protects your heart and vessels.
4. You become more even-tempered! Water-soluble fiber helps stabilize both blood sugar and mood.
5. It's perfect training food, because oats contain highly nutritious, quality protein.

15. HEMP POWDER/HEMP SEED
(if hulled: HEMP HEARTS)

Hemp is truly an all-purpose raw product. It provides us with many things, including clothing, paper, oil, seeds, powder, and hulled seeds (hearts). It's widely used as a food source, too. You can sprinkle hemp seeds over a salad, make tasty hemp mylk, or boost the protein content of your energy bars and smoothies with hemp powder. If you're looking for a really good oil supplement, hemp oil is a fantastic option.

> **TOP 5 REASONS WHY YOU SHOULD EAT HEMP PRODUCTS**
> **1.** Develop stronger muscles. Hemp contains all the essential amino acids needed for increased muscle growth.
> **2.** Get radiant hair and skin! We have to lubricate our body from the inside; good fats impart a fresh glow to both hair and skin.
> **3.** The fatty acid combination found in hemp products has a positive effect on our cognitive function.
> **4.** The fatty acids Omega 3, 6, and 9 in hemp seeds help to lubricate our blood vessels and keep them in good working order.
> **5.** They hasten recovery. In order to train we must also be able to recover, and hemp helps us with our exercise load and as well as our ability to recover after physical exertion.

16. ALMONDS

We typically find almonds in the nut category, even though it is in fact a stone fruit—a drupe—with a seed inside. Whatever we call them, they're delicious! And healthy! You can make mylk and almond butter, and you can use them as a base for balls and bars, or in raw food burgers and crackers.

> **TOP 5 REASONS WHY YOU SHOULD EAT ALMONDS**
> **1.** They protect the body's cells. The Vitamin E in almonds prolongs the lifespan of body cells.
> **2.** The good fats in almonds have a positive impact on our hormonal system because they contain the amino acid tryptophan, which is needed to produce serotonin.
> **3.** Almonds contain polyphenols that lower cholesterol, which in turn lowers the risk for cardiovascular disease.
> **4.** Calcium strengthens our bones and teeth; you'll get lots of calcium in almonds.
> **5.** Almonds strengthen the immune system! The mineral zinc reinforces the body's immune system.

17. CHIA SEEDS

Chia seeds were a staple food of the Mayan culture; they were consumed first and foremost before long treks and prior to going into battle. Chia seeds came to our attention and became popular in today's Western world thanks to a book on running. Since then, chia seeds have found their way to—and feel right at home in—most pantries; one year 'chia pudding' topped the list of most-frequently Googled terms. Maybe you've noticed how good they make you feel? See below to learn more about all their beneficial effects and you'll understand why!

I really only have one recommendation when it comes to chia seeds, and that is: eat them! Keep the amount to about 3 tablespoons per day, and don't forget that the seeds increase 5 to 10 times in volume once they come into contact with liquids, so it's preferable to soak them before eating them.

I always bring chia seeds with me on my travels. They're so easy to just mix into a cup of tea, a glass of juice, or in a smoothie. They keep me satiated for a good long while and provide me with lots of nutrition.

> **TOP 5 REASONS WHY YOU SHOULD EAT CHIA SEEDS**
> **1.** One product of the combination of nutrients present in chia seeds is stronger nails and great hair!
> **2.** Chia seeds are also jokingly referred to as 'the dieter's best friend,' since they provide ample satiety despite their low calorie content.
> **3.** They're small seeds packed with all the essential amino acids, fatty acids, antioxidants, fiber, vitamins, and minerals—small and complete!
> **4.** The digestive system is happy thanks to their fiber content and the gel they develop.
> **5.** The water-soluble fibers in chia seeds make them absorb about 10 times their own weight in water, which helps balance out blood sugar.

18. COCONUT OIL

The different parts of the coconut palm—fruits, leaves, sap, and flowers—provide us with plenty of food. We get coconut flour, coconut milk, coconut cream, shredded coconut, coconut butter, coconut oil, coconut syrup, coconut palm sugar, coconut alcohol, coconut water, and coconut flakes—all from the same tree. Even the trunk and the leaves play separate but important functions in daily life in countries where the palms grow.

All the different coconut products have different nutritional profiles. It is very simple to add coconut oil to your daily diet, and it can be used in both cooking and baking.

TOP 5 REASONS WHY YOU SHOULD EAT COCONUT OIL
1. The fatty acids in coconut oil suppress viruses.
2. The medium-chain fatty acids in coconut oil have an antimicrobial effect on different fungal diseases that can occur in the body.
3. Bacteria does not like coconut oil, so the oil is antibacterial. Take some oil as a preventive measure, or increase your dose if you're sick.
4. The fat in coconut oil raises our metabolism of fat and stabilizes our weight. A tablespoon of oil can quell cravings for sweets in the afternoon.
5. Coconut oil has a probiotic effect and strengthens the intestinal flora.

19. HONEY

A teaspoon of honey can replace what would have been a bag of candy or other sweets. Honey contains saccharose—sucrose—but you also get added nutrients: vitamins, antioxidants, and minerals. Thanks to an enzyme provided by the honeybees, sucrose is transformed into fructose and glucose. Enjoy the honey without heating it up, or you will lose all its nutrients. If you add honey to your tea, the tea's temperature should not exceed 95°F–104°F (35°C–40°C).

Vegans who eat honey are called beegans. However, you can replace honey with yacon, maple syrup, or agave syrup if you wish to avoid honey.

Bee pollen is flower pollen caught on the back legs of bees. Bee pollen is considered the most nutrient-dense food of all; it even accompanies astronauts into space.

TOP 5 REASON WHY YOU SHOULD EAT HONEY

1. Honey boosts our health—it contains lactic acid bacteria, which is good for our intestines.
2. It's good after a workout! Instead of an energy drink, honey can help us restore our body's balance.
3. Honey contributes to more restful sleep. Research has shown that if you ingest 2–4 teaspoons of honey before going to bed, you experience better recovery and have lower levels of stress hormones when you wake up.
4. Honey is referred to as nature's own antibiotic. It has great antibacterial properties and is a cough suppressant.
5. Honey is a natural beauty product; making your own face mask with honey is both fun and tasty. Research has also shown that sores heal faster when honey has been applied.

It's good to fortify yourself with superfoods during menopause, as they will help balance out your hormonal changes. Maca powder and cacao powder are beneficial due to their antioxidant and mineral content, and leafy greens are rich in the mineral magnesium, which affects the hormonal system. It's also important to consume raw ingredients that are rich in Vitamins B and C.

20. MACA POWDER

Maca powder is an adaptogen. The root from which the powder is extracted can survive the cold, heat, floods, and droughts. And just as it can adapt to different climates, it can also adapt to the preconditions we humans exhibit. It can help balance the hormonal and nervous systems to enable us to handle the stress that external factors can create within us.

TOP 5 REASONS WHY YOU SHOULD EAT MACA POWDER

1. Maca is rich in zinc, which affects our hormonal balance and our sex drive; the latter effect is the reason why maca's nickname is "Peruvian Viagra."
2. It provides a kick! Maca can give you a real jolt of energy, so bear that in mind if you take it at night.
3. Maca can help you improve in whatever you're trying to achieve.
4. You can use maca to stimulate your recovery after training.
5. Since maca is an adaptogen, it can help you think more clearly and keenly.

21. RAW CACAO POWDER

Regular cocoa or raw cacao powder? What's the difference, really? If you have a package of each item in front of you, you can easily tell one from the other. If you've begun using raw cacao powder in balls, bars, smoothies, and mylkshakes, you will have noticed the smoothness and soft flavor it imparts. From a nutritional standpoint, all the antioxidants and fatty acids are preserved in the raw cacao.

TOP 5 REASONS WHY YOU SHOULD EAT RAW CACAO

1. You will feel happier! The amino acid tryptophan, which affects serotonin levels and can make us feel cheery, is found in cacao.
2. Cacao is rich in magnesium, a mineral that makes us feel more relaxed.
3. Cacao is one of the world's principal sources of antioxidants, and is therefore considered a rejuvenating food.
4. Cacao is rich in iron, which is especially important for women in their childbearing years.
5. It gives you pep! Cacao powder contains caffeine, but at a low dose—approximately 1/20th of that of coffee.

22. SAUERKRAUT

Sauerkraut is like a real miracle worker for your health and well-being. As little as a tablespoon per day can affect your health in positive ways. It's easier than you think to make sauerkraut at home. Fermentation is a biological process that preserves and increases the vital processes in food and bacteria. You can easily find information online on how to ferment food.

Sauerkraut juice can be bought in cartons, to be used as complement to sauerkraut or instead of it—if you don't like sauerkraut. Drink a glass of the juice before your meal to improve the absorption of your food, and to increase the amount of good bacteria in your intestines.

TOP 5 REASONS WHY YOU SHOULD EAT SAUERKRAUT
1. It's easy to digest! Regular cabbage can be real tough for the stomach to break down, whereas with sauerkraut, digestion has already started through fermentation.
2. It helps fight infections. Your immune system will be more powerful if you have good bacterial flora in your digestive tract.
3. Cabbage is known for its high Vitamin C content; sauerkraut contains even more of it.
4. It's affordable! It's one of the cheapest superfoods you can eat and prepare at home.
5. In Russia, lactic fermentation belongs to their sources of rejuvenation—their "fountain of youth." Let sauerkraut become your source of rejuvenation, too.

23. ALGAE

Algae are one of the most nutritionally dense raw ingredients on Earth, and they're extremely good for you.

Algae are also an environmentally sound source of protein. Spirulina and Chlorella are called miracle algae because they contain lots of cholorphyll, vitamins, and minerals; they even help to stabilize blood sugar and can blunt cravings for sweets. They can be found in powder and in pill form.

TOP 5 REASONS WHY YOU SHOULD EAT ALGAE

1. They rid the body of dangerous heavy metals. Alginates in the algae detoxify the body.
2. Algae are rich in Vitamin Bs, which are good for proper nervous system function.
3. It's a great workout food! Algae are high in protein.
4. Do you suffer from hypothyroidism? Algae contain a natural form of iodine.
5. They're rich in minerals! Iron, copper, and magnesium are vital minerals for us. They make us more alert, protect our cells, and have a positive effect on our muscles and nerves.

24. CINNAMON

A sprinkling of cinnamon on your cereal? Cinnamon has so many other benefits besides adding nice flavor that it gives us all the more reason to sprinkle more of it and more often than just over our oatmeal. Cinnamon is harvested by hand, and a special technique is used to peel the bark from its trunk. Cinnamon varies widely in quality and taste; the best comes from Sri Lanka (Ceylon), and is sweet and flavorful. It's recommended that you consume at least one teaspoon of cinnamon per day. Add it to your food or mix it into your drink!

TOP 5 REASONS WHY YOU SHOULD EAT CINNAMON
1. Cinnamon warms you and improves your body's circulation.
2. It reduces urges for sweets! A cup of cinnamon tea kills the craving and balances blood sugar.
3. Cinnamon enhances the taste of sweet, so you can use less sweetener.
4. It keeps you healthy! Cinnamon is rich in antioxidants that strengthen the immune system.
5. Cinnamon stimulates the digestion.

25. GREEN TEA & MATCHA TEA

Matcha tea comes from Japan. It's made from the very first tender leaves of the tea plant, which are dried and then ground by stone grinding wheels. Matcha contains more antioxidants and chlorophyll than regular green tea. Green tea may be regarded as cleansing, and so it's best to drink it early or later in the morning. If you cold brew your tea, the amount of caffeine will be less and there won't be any acrid or bitter taste. You can't cold brew Matcha tea like regular green tea leaves.

You can read more about how to cold brew tea on page 91.

You can read more about how to cold brew tea on page 91.

TOP 5 REASONS WHY YOU SHOULD DRINK GREEN TEA AND MATCHA TEA

1. They boost your health with lots of antioxidants.
2. They contain catechins, which are said to prevent cancer.
3. They speed up metabolism!
4. They make you more alert—but not due to any unnecessary caffeine. Matcha does have a higher caffeine content than regular green tea.
5. Green tea can have a positive impact on weight loss, primarily yerba mate, a South American herb that helps curtail hunger pangs.

RECIPES

All the recipes are based on the basic 25 raw super ingredients. You'll always be able to put something tasty, wholesome, and health-boosting together if you have them on hand at home. You'll find most of these ingredients at your local grocery store.

SHELF LIFE AND STORAGE

Bowls/puddings/cereals will keep for about 24 hours in the refrigerator.

Smoothies/beverages/ mylkshakes will keep for about 24 hours in the refrigerator.

Balls/bars will keep for about 2 weeks in the refrigerator, or for several months in the freezer.

Light lunches/dinners will keep in the refrigerator for 24 hours.

Nice cream will keep in the freezer for a few months if stored in an airtight container.

KITCHEN EQUIPMENT

You'll be perfectly fine with an immersion blender and its (slightly larger) container; if you own a blender with stronger motor or a food processor, that's a bonus. Results may vary depending on which piece of equipment you use. Start out with the tools you already have.

Immersion blender and container. The immersion blender comes with its own mixing bowl. It's preferable to choose one with a slightly larger bowl.

Electric mixer/blender. They come in a range of brands, quality levels, and prices. In brief, we can say that the stronger the motor, the better the end result. If you use the mixer regularly, maybe even daily, it's well worth investing in a higher-priced model. You'll use the blender to make smoothies, mylks, Nice creams, and dressings.

Food processor. A simple food processor usually works very well and gets good results. You'll use it to make, for example, balls, bars, and Nice cream.

GLOSSARY

Mylk is vegetable-based milk.

Nice cream is what we call ice cream when it's vegetable-based and without any added white sugar. It's nice for you, nice for the animals, and nice for our planet.

Zoodles are noodles made from vegetables. You'll make them with a spiralizer or a serrated root vegetable peeler.

Bowls, for when you serve the food in—bowls.

Superfood snacks are good to go—and super easy to brown bag!

BOWLS, PUDDINGS, AND GRAINS

Smart food in a small bowl

BOWLS

A bowl is really a smoothie without a lot of liquid, and by including frozen berries you get a consistency that's closer to yogurt. You can top your bowl in a thousand different ways—and it looks beautiful, too! The acai bowl is a classic bowl made with frozen acai; the round acai pucks can be found in the frozen foods section at the grocery store. But don't limit yourself to acai—try out different ingredients. If you want a cold bowl, just use frozen berries or fruits; otherwise, add defrosted or fresh berries.

The great thing is that you can top your bowl with what you need, or you can just enjoy the bowl as is. If you're in training, you may wish to include extra protein by adding in hemp protein and topping it with goji berries. If you feel a cold coming on, top the bowl with bee pollen and add in a little extra ginger. If you want to make the bowl more filling, incorporate some chia seeds and oats. The variations are limitless! That the ingredients are put through the blender or food processor eases the digestive process.

If you want to turn a bowl into a smoothie, simply add more liquid, but your sense of satiety will be greater if you eat the concoction with a spoon rather than drink it down; there's even research proving this to be the case. It'll be even more filling if you add a topping.

PUDDINGS

The jelly that forms when you soak chia seeds is responsible for creating the mouthfeel of pudding. Read more about these super seeds on page 40, and I promise that you'll run to the store to buy some, if you don't already have some chia seeds at home. They're absolutely crammed full of good-for-you-ness! You'll definitely become dishy from eating a dish of chia pudding! The liquid base for chia pudding can vary: you can use water, mylk, juice, tea, coconut water, or any other liquid that you like.

Chia seeds are ideal on-the-go food. They take up little space, provide long-lasting satiety, they're amazingly nutritious, and have a neutral flavor. When I travel I usually bring a jar of chia seeds, dried buckwheat, goji berries, and vanilla powder. When I'm hungry, I add some liquid, wait about 10 minutes, and my food is ready.

Chia pudding and overnight cereal require minimal effort to make, and you don't need any special tools. Just mix and enjoy!

GRAINS

Oatmeal is now all the rage, but what's rated even higher are grains or oats that have been soaked overnight—or at least for an hour or so—in liquid; try replacing the water with mylk. Soaking removes the phytins that act as the cereals' own preservative (so to speak) and which prevent the body from absorbing certain nutrients. Soaking also increases the nutritional value of the oats and helps us to digest them. And since you don't cook the grains, all their nutrients remain intact.

EXOTIC BROCCOLI BOWL
SERVES 2

Broccoli is green and contains chlorophyll—just like leafy greens. But broccoli also contains Vitamin C and other antioxidants. Together with pineapple's nutritional wholesomeness (the enzyme bromelain is great for the gut and fights inflammation), this is a real boost for your health.

5 fl oz (1½ dl) broccoli florets, fresh or frozen
8¾ oz (250 g) frozen pineapple or tropical fruit mix
6¾ fl oz (2 dl) coconut water
1 banana
1 avocado
A splash of freshly squeezed lemon juice

Cut the broccoli florets into smaller chunks. Blend all ingredients into a smooth texture.

5 tips to get going

Read through the recipes and put together a shopping list.

Purchase the ingredients.

Arrange fruit and vegetables attractively, and put up a dedicated superfood shelf in the pantry.

Dare yourself to follow a new recipe every day. See if you can get your best friend to join you in the challenge.

Just start! Take it one meal at a time.

SAM'S BOWL
SERVES 2

My husband Sam is a great source of inspiration to me. He taste-tests everything I prepare. When he declares that something tastes healthy, I know that it's more good-for-you than good to eat … but he still gamely finishes it! This is his own recipe for a bowl, and it is both healthy and tasty. Chlorophyll and sprouting life force from the pea sprouts, good fats from the avocado, and creamy sweetness from a banana will get you set for a busy day.

3 bananas, frozen or fresh
1 packet pea sprouts, approx. 3½ oz (100g)
1 avocado
A pinch of vanilla powder
TOPPING:
2 tbsp goji berries
2 tbsp hemp seeds
2 tbsp bee pollen

Peel and slice the bananas—put them in a plastic bag and freeze them if you wish to use frozen bananas. You can blend the frozen bananas if you have a powerful blender. If not, defrost the fruit for 10 minutes first. Mix the bananas with the pea sprouts, avocado, and vanilla powder until you have a creamy consistency. Top with goji berries, hemp seeds, and bee pollen.

Did you know that goji means happy? If you eat goji berries, you'll stay both healthy and happy!

ACAI BOWL
SERVES 2

The classic acai bowl is made with pureed fruit from frozen acai 'pucks', which you can find in the frozen foods section of your grocery store. To prepare a chilled version of this bowl, simply defrost the puck a little, or else defrost the acai puck completely in the bowl, and mix it with bananas. It's perfectly fine to use avocado instead of banana to make a slightly less sweet purée. And if you boost the bowl with chia seeds, you not only increase its nutrient content, you also end up with a more satisfying and heartier texture.

   The acai berry comes from a tree in Brazil, where it is called the Tree of Life. The berry is loaded with antioxidants and healthy fats—perfect for a beautiful complexion.

7 oz (200 g) frozen acai berries, or 1 tbsp acai powder
   and 7 oz (200 g) frozen blueberries

3 bananas

2 tbsp chia seeds (optional)

TOPPING:

1 tbsp lucuma powder

2 tbsp dried mulberries

4 tbsp pomegranate seeds

2 sprigs of lemon balm

In a food processor, mix acai and banana to a smooth consistency. Add 2 tablespoons chia seeds, if desired. Pour the mixture into two bowls, dust with lucuma powder, sprinkle with mulberries and pomegranate seeds, and top with lemon balm.

BLUEBERRY BOWL
SERVES 2

It's difficult for me not to sneak in some leafy greens, even in a bowl. Spinach is good here because its flavor isn't overpowering, and when combined with the blueberries its color is not discernible. However, all the nutrients are in there! Chlorophyll and fiber from the spinach, fiber from the chia seeds, too, and antioxidants from both the chia seeds and the blueberries. It is, quite simply, a terrific health boost. Make it even better with some blueberry powder, if you like.

2 bananas

½ cup (1 dl) blueberries, frozen or defrosted

1 handful of green leaves

1 avocado

2 tbsp chia seeds

¼–½ cup (½–1 dl) water (optional)

1 tbsp blueberry powder (optional)

TOPPING:

¼ cup (½ dl) frozen blueberries

1 banana, sliced

Blend everything to a smooth puree. The chia seeds don't need to be soaked, they just add some firmness to the bowl if you let the mixture sit for a bit. Top the bowl with blueberries and banana.

FIG BOWL
SERVES 2

Figs are chock full of goodness. Dried figs have more concentrated sweetness and a higher sugar content, but still, they're a far superior alternative to regular table sugar and candy. And you'll get fiber, minerals, and vitamins in the bargain!

Soaking figs softens them, and a large quantity of the sugar created through the drying process dissolves in the soaking liquid. Dehydration increases the shelf life of the delicate fresh fig. Dried figs provide you with iron—a super vital mineral that helps the body transport oxygen. Many women and girls are deficient in iron. Figs also contain the minerals calcium, phosphorus, and magnesium, which build strong bones.

6 dried figs (soft or pre-soaked)

1 avocado

2 apples

Scant ½ cup frozen blueberries

1 tsp flaxseed oil or Udo's choice oil

¾" (2 cm) piece of ginger

3⅓–6¾ fl oz (1–2 dl) water (or use the soaking water from the figs)

TOPPING:

2 tbsp hemp seeds

1 tbsp bee pollen

2 fresh figs

Dried and soaked fruit contribute creaminess to a bowl. If the dried fruit is already soft you don't need to soak it. Some of the fruit's sugar disappears during soaking— dried fruit does have a higher concentration of sugar than its fresh counterpart. Drying is a natural conservation process. You can use the soaking water for diluting and sweetening purposes.

Soak the figs for about 8 hours. Peel the avocado and remove the stone. Core and cut the apples into chunks. Blend everything except topping ingredients to a smooth cream and pour into two bowls. Top with hemp seeds, bee pollen, and fresh figs cut into smaller chunks.

MANGO BOWL
WITH COCONUT
SERVES 2

My favorite topping, particularly with mango, is large coconut chips. They provide such wonderful crunch against the smooth cream. If you want an even creamier bowl, use coconut cream only. For a chilled version, use frozen mango.

3 bananas

4½ oz (125 g) frozen mango, or a scant ½ cup (1 dl) dried and soaked mango

6¾ fl oz (2 dl) (½ tin) coconut milk

A pinch of vanilla powder

Lemon oil or grated lemon peel (optional)

TOPPING:

1 sliced banana

12 fresh strawberries

2 tbsp raw coconut chips

Grated peel from one lemon

If you're using dehydrated mango, soak it in water for 2 to 8 hours. Blend all the ingredients (except toppings) to a smooth cream and pour into two bowls. Top with sliced banana and sliced strawberries, coconut chips, and grated lemon peel.

ANTIOXIDANTS & FREE RADICALS

Antioxidants are said to be the key to a long and healthy life, and it is an umbrella term for several different nutrients: minerals, vitamins, and what are referred to as bioactive compounds. What they have in common is a positive effect on health because they neutralize free radicals. Free radicals are created naturally when we breathe, but our lifestyle, sun exposure, smoking, and other factors influence the quantity of free radicals we generate.

Free radicals can cause damage—also called oxidative stress—to our cells. Oxidative stress is a type of cell breakdown that we can hinder by making sure we get enough antioxidants. So what we eat influences us to a significant degree!

Remember to eat fruits and vegetables in a wide range of colors. The more we mix the different colors, the better protected we are.

The rainbow colored diet = food rich in antioxidants = protection from oxidative stress ("rust") = a long and healthy life!

STRAWBERRY COCONUT YOGURT
SERVES 2

A kid-friendly and good vegetarian yogurt for newbies. It's beautiful and amazingly delicious! Good-for-you fats, antioxidants from the "super-berry" strawberry, naturally sweetened with dates. Psst—make some extra yogurt and pour it into ice cream molds and serve it as a refreshing and delicious frozen yogurt.

4 dates
15 strawberries, fresh or frozen
5 fl oz (1½ dl) coconut milk
2 bananas
A pinch of vanilla powder

TOPPINGS:
6 fresh strawberries
2 tbsp bee pollen

Remove the stones from the dates. In a food processor or blender, mix all the ingredients (except toppings) to a creamy consistency. Spoon into bowls and top with sliced fresh strawberries and bee pollen.

CRANBERRY BOWL
SERVES 2

Take this opportunity to use fresh berries when they're in season. You can also replace the cranberries with raspberries or other frozen berries for a bit of variety. If you want some extra fat, just add in coconut oil.

1 cup (2 dl) buckwheat, without hulls
1 cup (2 dl) fresh cranberries, or defrosted if frozen
1 avocado
1 tbsp honey
1 tbsp coconut oil (optional)
½ cup (1 dl) water or coconut water (optional)

SUGGESTED TOPPINGS:
Fresh or frozen cranberries
Dehydrated buckwheat
Liquid honey or yacon syrup

Soak the hulled buckwheat (it will swell when soaking) for 8 hours or overnight. Rinse the soaked buckwheat thoroughly in a fine-meshed sieve. Mix the buckwheat with the remaining ingredients (except toppings) in a food processor or blender until you have a creamy consistency. Spoon it in bowls and top with cranberries, dehydrated buckwheat (find out how to dehydrate buckwheat on p. 63), and the sweetener.

TRAINING BOWL

SERVES 2

To achieve good results from working out, the body needs to be replenished with good fuel.
Celery is perfect to use as a boost since it helps balance blood pressure, fights inflammation, and improves digestion. Of course, you can boost with berries, too.

3 stalks celery

5 fresh dates

1¼ cup (3 dl) almond mylk (see pp. 80–81)

2 avocados, peeled, pitted, and sliced

1 tbsp hemp protein powder

Some water (optional)

Cut the celery stalks into chunks. Remove the stones from the dates. In a food processor or blender, mix it all to a smooth consistency, and dilute with some water if needed.

BUCKWHEAT

Buckwheat gives bowls some added heft and fills you up more. Hulled buckwheat needs to soak for about 8 hours to release a type of dormant enzyme. At this point a thick, reddish liquid is created, which you need to rinse off thoroughly with lukewarm water. Continue by sprouting the kernels at room temperature for 2 days, or store them in the refrigerator to prolong the sprouting process and the kernels' shelf life. What's cool is that soaked and rinsed buckwheat can keep in the refrigerator for about 5 days. Remember to rinse the sprouts once a day. The buckwheat will then keep sprouting and grow a small tail, which means that it's even healthier for you. You can also dehydrate buckwheat in the oven or in a dehydrator.

HOW TO DEHYDRATE BUCKWHEAT

Soak the whole, hull-free buckwheat for 8 hours. Thoroughly rinse off the reddish liquid that has appeared. Leave the kernels to sprout for one day. Spread the kernels on a baking sheet lined with parchment paper, and slide them into an oven warmed to 115°F (45°C). Let the buckwheat dry for about 15 hours. This way you have activated and dehydrated the buckwheat, which will now keep for several months in an airtight jar. Dried buckwheat adds a nice crunch to balls, bars, and raw chocolate, as well as to bowl toppings.

You can add these toppings to your bowls:

Hemp seeds

Raw coconut chips

Activated and
dehydrated
buckwheat

Bee pollen

Dehydrated
mulberries

Cranberry powder

Fresh fruit and berries

Blueberry powder

Goji berries

CASHEW YOGURT

It sure sounds complex doesn't it? But if you make
a large batch of it once a week, you'll have enough
on hand for several days. You can eat it plain, mix it
into a smoothie, stir in berries for a yogurt, or enjoy
it with berries and sweetener as a decadent frozen
yogurt. The good bacteria in the probiotics capsules
create the yogurt's culture. When you add probiotics,
the yogurt 'comes to life.' That is excellent for the
stomach as well as all-around health!

   The basic recipe makes a neutral-tasting yogurt,
but why not add some vanilla powder for some extra
flavor? On the other hand, the neutral taste is good
if you wish to use the cashew yogurt as a raw food
version of tzatziki sauce.

2 cups (4½ dl) cashews
2 cups (4½ dl) lukewarm water
4 probiotics capsules
I tsp vanilla powder (optional)

In a blender, mix the cashews with the water. Open the
probiotics capsules and add the contents to the mixed
cashews with the optional vanilla powder, and mix
again. Pour the mixture into a glass bowl (do not use
a metal bowl, or the yogurt culture will not grow) and
cover it with a kitchen towel. Let the bowl sit at room
temperature for the day, or overnight, to let the process
begin. The yogurt will keep for up to a week in the
refrigerator, in a bowl or jar with a tight-fitting lid.

OVERNIGHT OATS
SERVES 2

I use high-quality naked oats in this recipe, but you can try using buckwheat, quinoa, or spelt flakes instead. The fiber will keep your blood sugar stable and you feel full longer.

1¼ cup (3 dl) rolled oats, preferably naked oats

2 cups + 2 tsp (5 dl) apple juice or water

A pinch of salt

3 tbsp sunflower seeds

3 tbsp goji berries

TOPPING:

1 apple

1 tsp ground cinnamon

1 tbsp coconut palm sugar (optional)

Soak the oats in apple juice or water, and add in a pinch of salt. Fold in the sunflower seeds and the goji berries. Let sit for 1 to 8 hours. Serve the bowl topped with an apple cut into chunks and the cinnamon. If you want to make the bowl sweeter, sprinkle the oat mix with some coconut palm sugar.

CHILI & CACAO CHIA
SERVES 2

We all have our favorite spices—cinnamon and cardamom are a couple of mine. But why not make a chili and cacao pudding? The chili doesn't just add heat, it also stabilizes blood sugar and boosts metabolism, and can help kick-start weight loss. Other suggested flavorings are dried ginger, nutmeg, and a pinch of saffron.

1¼ cup (3 dl) mylk

4 tbsp chia seeds

2 tsp raw cacao powder

½ tsp dried chili powder

1 tbsp honey

TOPPING:

Your choice of chopped nuts

Mulberries

Dried buckwheat (see p. 63)

Mix together all the ingredients for the pudding. Let it sit for at least 30 minutes, and top it with chopped nuts, mulberries, and dried buckwheat before serving.

OVERNIGHT OAT BOWL WITH CHIA SEEDS
SERVES 2

This is a real skier's breakfast; it's great for when you need to feel full over a long period of time! Both the chia seeds and rolled oats are packed with fiber. You'll get extra energy from the almond butter. You can read up on how to make your own almond butter on p. 141. You should season the bowl a bit more in wintertime with 1 teaspoon each of ground cardamom, cinnamon, and ginger.

1 cup (2 dl) rolled oats

3 tbsp chia seeds

2 cups (4 dl) mylk

3 tbsp grated coconut

A pinch of salt

Ground spices (optional)

TOPPING:

2 tbsp almond butter

4 tbsp fresh or frozen blueberries and raspberries

1 banana

Put everything (except toppings) together in a jar and stir to mix thoroughly. Let the mix sit for at least 30 minutes in the refrigerator, and serve with almond mylk and toppings.

CRANBERRY GRAINS WITH SWEET RAISINS
SERVES 2

It doesn't matter whether you steep the grains during the day or overnight. Prepare jars with the dry ingredients in advance, and add berries and water. You can sweeten the grains with honey or maple syrup at the table instead of adding coconut sugar to the mix.

1 (2 dl) grains, such as rolled oats, buckwheat or quinoa

1–1¼ cup (2–3 dl) water or almond mylk

A pinch of salt

1 cup (2 dl) cranberries, frozen or fresh

1 tbsp coconut palm sugar

1 tbsp raisins

TOPPING:

¼ cup (½ dl) pecans

1 tsp ground cardamom

Stir the grains with water or mylk (use the lesser quantity of either if you're using frozen berries, because the berries will produce liquid as they defrost) and the remaining ingredients, except toppings. Let the mix stand for 1 to 8 hours. Top the mix with chopped pecans and cardamom.

FRUIT SALAD
WITH CHIA SEEDS
SERVES 1

You can sprinkle chia seeds over yogurt, cereal, or bowls. When you sprinkle them over fruit salad, the liquid from the fruit will soak and 'dilute' the seeds. However, don't use more than 1 to 2 tablespoons of chia seeds per portion.

SUGGESTED FRUITS:

a banana

a nectarine

a pear

¾" (2 cm) piece of fresh ginger, grated

Cut the fruit into chunks, mix them together, and sprinkle with chia seeds.

CHIA PUDDING
WITH A BOOST
SERVES 2

Try making mylk from Brazil nuts; it goes extremely well with the other flavors. You can switch out or omit the lucuma powder. The topping will give you an extra boost.

1 cup (2 dl) mylk, made from Brazil nuts

1 cup (2 dl) water

2 tbsp chia seeds

2 tbsp lucuma powder

2 tsp blueberry powder

½ tbsp coconut palm sugar

TOPPING:

2 bananas

2 tbsp cacao nibs

2 tbsp dried mulberries

Mix together all the ingredients for the pudding, and let it sit for at least 30 minutes. Mix it thoroughly before serving. Top the pudding with sliced banana, cacao nibs, and dried mulberries.

CHIA SEEDS WITH
POMEGRANATE
SERVES 2

Chia fresca, a popular drink in South America, is made from chia seeds mixed with water, lime juice, and some type of sweetener. I made a fresh, pumped up version of the drink that includes pomegranate seeds and coconut water. Vary the amount of liquid depending on if you want to make a chia drink or a pudding. Sweeten it with honey, if you prefer.

2 tbsp chia seeds

2 cups (4 dl) coconut water

½ cup (1 dl) pomegranate seeds, frozen

Mix the chia seeds and the coconut water, and stir in the pomegranate seeds. Let sit for at least 30 minutes before serving.

CHIA PUDDING
WITH BERRIES
SERVES 2

This is really the simplest snack or breakfast. Only three ingredients, and you have a meal packed with nutrients that counteract aging and keep skin soft! The frozen berries will defrost as the chia seeds soak.

2 cups (4 dl) mylk

4 tbsp chia seeds

½ cup (1 dl) berries—raspberries, blueberries, or blackberries, for example

For suggested toppings, see p. 64.

Mix mylk with the chia seeds and fold in the berries. Let stand for at least 30 minutes. Top or sweeten if you so wish.

SMOOTHIES, MYLKSHAKES, AND DRINKS

Perfect snacks, simple to put together, easy to bring along

Smoothies are a classic snack—simple to make and easy to bring along. You can also add variety depending on what you already have at home—sometimes by using lots of leafy greens, other times bringing out a fruitier side, or going decadent with cacao and something sweet. The simplest way for you to prepare a smoothie is to use a blender, because it shreds fiber very finely. This will make it easier for you to consume lots of fresh, raw ingredients.

Go for fresh bananas; if you've used frozen, you'll want to drink it immediately.

You can use different types of liquids for your base in a smoothie; coconut water and green tea are my personal favorites. For a more filling drink, use almond mylk. Chia seeds will also provide greater satiety, and you don't necessarily need to soak them first.

Beverages make excellent snacks, either as accompaniments to other food or as a treat when a craving hits instead of real hunger; you don't always have to eat a snack. Juices and drinks are perfect replenishments that don't overburden your body with fiber, since their nutrients are absorbed directly.

KALE SMOOTHIE
SERVES 2

Does it still sound weird to drink kale? Once you've tested this smoothie, you'll be wondering what took you so long to try it. Kale is more full-bodied than delicate leafy greens.

My kids like apple juice as the liquid base because it's a little sweeter. Add a teaspoon of Spirulina if you like—it will make the smoothie greener and more nutritious.

2–3 branches of kale
4" (10 cm) English (hothouse) cucumber
½ cup (1 dl) dried and reconstituted mango or
    4½ oz (125 g) frozen mango, defrosted
¾" (2 cm) piece of fresh ginger
1¼ cup (3 dl) water or apple juice
1 tsp Spirulina powder (optional)

Strip the kale leaf from the stem and cut it into pieces. Cut the cucumber into chunks. Process all ingredients in a blender (or use an immersion blender) until you have a smooth texture.

SUPERFOOD SMOOTHIE
MAKES 1 GLASS

A sprinkle of this powder and a dash of another powder—that's often what my morning smoothies look like. Then I feel charged up in the best way for the rest of the day. I often make a larger batch and save some for the afternoon, so my snack is already made when I feel hungry.

Different super-powders have different qualities; oftentimes their flavors match up well and they reinforce each other nutritionally. Mesquite is a powder that comes from an elongated bean. It's low on the GI index, has high protein content, and is rich in minerals that stabilize blood sugar and prolong feelings of satiety. If you want to make your smoothie thicker and more filling, simply add in some soaked buckwheat.

Approx. 1¼ cup (3 dl) almond mylk
1 tbsp chia seeds
½ tbsp raw carob powder or raw cacao powder
½ tbsp mesquite powder
½ tbsp lucuma powder
½ tbsp honey or yacon syrup (or add more to taste)

Process all ingredients in a blender (or use an immersion blender) until you have a smooth texture.

SPIRULINA SMOOTHIE
MAKES 4 GLASSES

A rehydrating and revitalizing beverage! I recommend swapping all the water out for coconut water if it's hot outside. Coconut water supplies the body with vital electrolytes that restore salt and mineral levels as you sweat. Spirulina has a cooling effect on the body. It also provides you with vital minerals, chlorophyll, and the fatty acid GLA, which can be helpful with PMS (premenstrual syndrome), skin problems, and eczema.

2 pears
½ cup (1 dl), approx. 1/3 fennel bulb
1¾ cup (4 dl) spinach—approx. 3½ oz (100 g)
1 cup (2 dl) water + 1 cup (2 dl) coconut water
2 bananas
2 tsp spirulina powder
¾ cup (1½ dl) frozen raspberries
some freshly squeezed lemon or lime juice
½" (1 cm) piece of fresh ginger

Cut the pears and fennel into chunks. Mix them together with the spinach, water, and coconut water. Add the remaining ingredients and blend to a smooth consistency.

SMOOTHIE WITH MACA AND GOJI BERRIES
SERVES 2

Our body requires antioxidants to protect itself against free radicals, which affect aging. Both raw cacao and goji berries feature extremely high levels of antioxidants, and along with a boost of maca powder you'll also get all the amino acids you need. In other words, it's both tasty and healthy! You can replace the banana with avocado, and maybe add something for sweetness. If you want, you can soak the goji berries for 30 minutes to make them easier to blend. Then, use the soaking water and reduce the amount of coconut water accordingly.

1¾ cup (4 dl) coconut water
1 tbsp raw maca powder
4 tbsp goji berries
2 frozen or fresh bananas

Blend all the ingredients to a smooth consistency.

—————

Supplementing with superfoods is good for both recovery and end results when it comes to training. What you need depends on your goal, whether it's to improve your overall health, become more flexible, or to build stronger muscles. The leafy greens that are rich in chlorophyll increase the uptake of oxygen, which is good in all types of exercise.

For extra protein

Boost with hemp powder or other vegetarian protein powder.

For extra carbohydrates

Add extra fruit, oats, or buckwheat

For extra flexibility

Eat foods that keep your joints supple. Turmeric, which contains curcumin, counteracts stiff joints, and coconut oil, which lubricates the joints, are two prime examples.

To get ready for a training session

Raw cacao powder, maca powder, or green tea.

The perfect recovery beverage

Blend 1 tbsp honey, 2 stalks of celery, 2 tbsp of freshly squeezed lemon juice, and coconut water or plain water. Strain through a mesh strainer.

SOFT GREEN SMOOTHIE WITH ALMOND MYLK

MAKES 2 GLASSES

Creamy smoothies—I love them! With just enough sweetness from the pear and creaminess from the avocado, this smoothie is so soothing for the stomach. If you're active and want a boost, you can add in some hemp powder, rice protein, or rice bran.

½ hothouse (English) cucumber

I pear

I avocado

3 handfuls of spinach, approx. 2½ oz (70 g)

1¾ cup (4 dl) almond mylk

I tbsp freshly squeezed lemon juice

I handful of fresh basil

Cut the cucumber and the pear into chunks. Scoop out the avocado. Blend all the ingredients to a smooth texture.

You'll need more carbohydrates (fruit, buckwheat, and oats are good), more protein (an extra protein shake!), and leafy greens for extra iron and calcium, if you're pregnant or breastfeeding. To build more power you can boost with cacao, maca, and green tea. You don't need to eat for two, but you will need to have enough strength for two!

MYLK

Vegetable-based milk is typically called mylk, so those of you who wish to avoid animal products will easily know what it's all about. I think the name of the new milk is cool; and it emphasizes how words can be created and go on to become as self-evident as the word 'milk'.

It is really simple to make your own mylk. This ensures that you're 100% sure of what's in it, and you don't need to carry heavy grocery bags. Also, store-bought milk usually doesn't contain that much of the original raw ingredient, which means that sometimes you're just bringing home expensive water. With a fine-mesh strainer or nut-milk bag, you can make your own milk in a few minutes.

And you can use the residue from making the mylk as the base for raw food balls!

SOAKING NUTS

It's best to soak nuts and seeds for about 8 hours. This awakens their life force and increases their nutritional value, and enables you to digest them more readily.

You can vary their flavors and use different sweeteners, but here is my basic recipe. You can, of course, omit the salt and vanilla powder if you wish.

Almonds
Hazelnuts (Filberts)
Brazil nuts
Cashews
Tigernuts
Hemp seed (hemp hearts)

NUT/SEED MYLK

1 cup (2 dl) nuts/seeds
1 quart (1 liter) water
A pinch of salt
Two pinches of vanilla powder

Soak the nuts/seeds, if you wish. Process
all the ingredients in a blender. Place a
fine-meshed sieve over a deep bowl, or
use a nut-milk bag, for draining the mylk.
Pour the mylk into bottles and keep them
refrigerated. Mylk made with soaked nuts/
seeds has a shelf life of 2 days, non-soaked,
up to 3–4 days.

MYLKSHAKE WITH BERRIES
MAKES 1 GLASS

With some extra oats your mylkshake gains volume and becomes more filling, and you load up on carbohydrates.

1 cup (2 dl) mylk
½ cup (1 dl) water
½ cup (1 dl) mixed berries, fresh or frozen
½ banana
½ cup (1 dl) rolled oats
1 tbsp blueberry powder

Mix all the ingredients in a blender to a smooth consistency.

SPICE MYLK
MAKES 1 GLASS

During wintertime, spices are great for raising body heat and increasing circulation. You can also warm the mylk in a saucepan till it's lukewarm; use your finger to check the temperature—it works great. Spiced mylk is the perfect snack when you're craving something but aren't really hungry.

1 cup (2 dl) mylk
pinch of vanilla powder
½ tsp ground cinnamon
scant ¼ tsp ground cardamom
½ tbsp honey

Mix everything together in a cup or in a saucepan. Drink as is, or warm it carefully till it reaches body temperature.

CREAMY CACAO MYLK WITH BUCKWHEAT
MAKES 2 GLASSES

This recipe is kind of like chocolate milk. If you want it lukewarm, just add some warm water. Cinnamon also helps warm the body from within. Sometimes it's nice to have something lukewarm! Buckwheat provides good satiety and contains complete protein, so it's perfect if you are physically active! You can read about how to soak buckwheat on page 63.

1 cup (2 dl) whole, de-hulled buckwheat
4 dates
1¾ cup (4 dl) mylk
1 cup (2 dl) water
2 tbsp raw cacao powder
1 tsp ground cinnamon
A pinch of salt

Soak the buckwheat for about 8 hours and rinse it thoroughly. Pit the dates. Process all the ingredients in a blender to a smooth consistency.

GOJI & ALMOND MYLKSHAKE
MAKES 2 GLASSES

This is a mylkshake that you can easily freeze to turn it into delicious nice cream. If you want a cold shake, use frozen banana, or frozen strawberries. Goji berries are good for your eyesight, and strawberries counteract the harmful effects of cholesterol. By all means, boost with some bracing maca powder, too!

1¼ (3 dl) almond mylk
1 tbsp goji berries
½ cup (1 dl) frozen strawberries
1 banana
1 tbsp maca powder (optional)
1 tbsp honey for added sweetness (optional)

Run all the ingredients in a blender to a smooth consistency.

8 tips on how to incorporate superfoods every day

Invite your friends for a raw food 'coffee' break.

Try abstaining from sugar for one month, and replacing it with raw food snacks and natural sweeteners.

Do you exercise? Test the powers of hemp and/or rice protein powders.

Make fruit leathers, balls, and nice cream— maybe together with the kids?

Drink one green smoothie per day—how do you feel after a few weeks?

Enjoy a raw foods breakfast—give yourself a clean start for 14 days.

Learn more about food's wholesome qualities, and then you'll want even more food with superpowers.

Choose a new super raw ingredient per day for the next 25 days. Read about each raw ingredient and try out a new recipe.

THE PERFECT MATCHA LATTE
MAKES 1 CUP

You can make the perfect matcha latte at home with a blender; you'll get a delicious, fluffy foam. Try it—I know you'll like it! For best results, use the white almond butter, or replace it with unsalted cashew butter. You can use almond mylk or other vegetable-based milk, but then you should omit the nut butter and the water.

1 tsp matcha powder
1 tsp honey for extra sweetness (optional)
1 tbsp white almond butter
1 cup (2 dl) water at 158°F (70°C) (or almond mylk)

Put the matcha powder, honey, and almond butter in the blender. Add water, and mix.

Cucumber as a snack?

Indeed, it's truly the only thing you need! Cucumber rehydrates the body, restores salt and mineral levels, and provides you with chlorophyll. It curbs cravings for sweets and clears your head.

———————

Eat the cucumber 'as is.'

Juice it.

Mix it in a blender and strain.

Grate the cucumber and press out all the liquid. Mix the cucumber with cashew yogurt (without vanilla powder) and stir in some garlic powder or a finely crushed garlic clove, salt, and black pepper. Voila, tzatziki sauce!

Can you get cucumbers affordably in the summer? If so, juice them and freeze the juice in ice cube trays.

CARROT JUICE

Carrot juice is incredibly healthy for you! You can extract about ½ quart (½ liter) of juice from 2¼ lbs (1 kg) carrots, and you don't have to chew but get the same benefits as if you did. Of course, the fiber in carrots fills an important function, but if you eat nutritious food the rest of the time you'll get all the fiber you need anyway. Add a splash of oil to your carrot juice, since it helps the body absorb beta carotene. A few drops of lemon juice act like a natural preservative.

2¼ lbs (1 kg) carrots
1¼" (3 cm) piece of fresh ginger
1 tsp liquid coconut oil
1 tbsp lemon juice (optional)

Wash the carrots if they're organic, otherwise peel them. Process the carrots with the ginger in a centrifugal juicer. Or, if you have a blender with a strong motor, you can mix the carrots with the ginger and 1 cup (2 dl) of water instead, then strain the juice through a fine-meshed sieve or a nut-milk bag. Stir in the coconut oil before serving.

COLD-BREWED GREEN TEA

Cold-brewed tea is my favorite beverage! Green tea doesn't get as bitter as when it is brewed warm, and I feel just sufficiently energized from it, since its caffeine doesn't have as much of an impact. If you enjoy lukewarm tea, fill your cup halfway with cold-brewed tea and add warm water to it.

1 tbsp green tea
1 quart water

Mix the tea leaves with the water inside a bottle. Let it steep at room temperature or in the refrigerator for about 4 to 8 hours.

JAPANESE CHERRY TEA

There's a type of tea that is difficult to find—Japanese cherry tea. I like it a lot so I make my own.

Add about 10 cherries to a quart of green tea that's cold-brewing in the refrigerator, in order to get the flavor and the nutrients from the fruit. You can strain out the fruit, or serve them in the tea.

ICED GREEN TEA

Mix some cold-brewed tea with lemon juice, a piece of ginger, honey or coconut palm sugar, and a few ice cubes. If your blender's motor isn't powerful enough to crush ice cubes, pour the tea into a glass with ice cubes.

CINNACINO

MAKES 1 CUP

Cinnamon luxury! Cinnacino is like a cappuccino, with cinnamon to make you feel warm if you eat a raw-food meal. It helps to stabilize blood sugar and will also stand in for a sweet treat after the meal. You can make it with either warm or cold water. Here, I use white almond butter or unsalted cashew butter.

1¾ cup (4 dl) water
1 tbsp nut butter
½ tbsp coconut palm sugar
3 tsp ground cinnamon

Heat up the water if you want a warm Cinnacino. Mix water, nut butter, coconut palm sugar, and cinnamon in a blender.

CINNAMON TEA

After a meal, or in the afternoon, I usually start craving something sweet. When it's more of a craving and not true hunger, cinnamon tea works wonders. You can warm up either some water or almond mylk, and stir in 1 teaspoon of ground cinnamon right into the cup. You can even simmer cinnamon sticks and strain off the cinnamon water, refrigerate it, and serve it with ice cubes for cinnamon-flavored iced tea.

LICORICE TEA

Licorice is a root and also a medicinal plant—it's black gold. If you have low blood pressure, licorice can help to raise it; so if you already have high blood pressure, you'll need to use caution when consuming licorice. Licorice can even provide cough relief and be a laxative; it's also an anti-inflammatory agent in the body. As an added bonus, licorice can boost your metabolism and regulate appetite, usually when taken as raw licorice tablets.

1 licorice root or ¼ cup (½ dl) finely chopped licorice
    root or 2 tsp licorice powder
1 quart (1 liter) water

Bring the water and the root to a boil and let boil for about 10 minutes. Strain the liquid. It's also fine to simply heat the water and stir in the licorice powder. Drink the beverage warm, or chill it to make iced tea and serve it with lemon and coconut palm sugar. Measure half a sliced lemon and 2 tablespoons of coconut palm sugar or honey per quart of tea.

PEPPERMINT HONEY WITH CACAO

Honey is delicious in its own right, but it becomes pure candy when you mix it with peppermint oil and cacao powder. One teaspoon can replace a piece of dark chocolate, or be made into a delicious beverage. It also makes a perfect hostess gift!

Peppermint oil is a highly concentrated form of peppermint—it is said that one drop of oil is the equivalent of 10 to 25 cups of peppermint tea, depending on its concentration. As an oil, this medicinal plant is used to ward off headaches, settle a fever, and aid digestion.

1 lb 2 oz (500 g) honey
3–5 drops peppermint oil
7 tbsp raw cacao powder

In a bowl, mix the honey with the peppermint oil and the cacao powder, then pour it all back into the honey jar. Use 1 or 2 teaspoons in a cup of warm water or warm mylk.

A QUICK CUP OF CHOCOLATE—INSTANT CHOCOLATE DRINK POWDER

Ready-to-mix chocolate drink powder can really make your day easier. Instead having to stand around mixing up a batch from several bags every time, you can make your own delicious pre-made mixture, completely free of white sugar.

CHOCOLATE MIXTURE:
3 tbsp raw cacao powder
1 tbsp lucuma powder
2 tbsp coconut palm sugar

Mix the ingredients and store them in a jar with a tight-fitting lid.

CHOCOLATE BEVERAGE:
1 tbsp nut butter, see p. 141
1¼ cup (3 dl) warm water
1 tbsp chocolate mixture

Blend the ingredients or whisk them together in a large cup.

ADDITIONALLY, I BOOST MY OWN CHOCOLATE MIX WITH:

• Maca powder—See p. 45.
• Reishi powder—Reishi is a medicinal mushroom that contains a wide range of minerals and vitamins, such as magnesium, potassium, calcium, and zinc.
• Mesquite powder is rich in fiber and protein, and even with its sweet taste, its GI index is low. Mesquite powder is rich in calcium.
• Carob powder. A cacao replacement rich in calcium and caffeine-free.

ICE CREAM– NICE CREAM

Vegetarian ingredients without artificial colors or refined white sugar

Ice cream is a refreshing and slightly indulgent snack that doesn't have to be loaded with sugar—at all. Ice cream made with vegetarian ingredients and without artificial colors or refined white sugar is called nice cream. A true health boost!

I use nut or almond butters in the recipes, since this makes the nice cream fuller-bodied and more like a cream-based ice cream. You can omit them if you'd like a lighter version of nice cream—more like a sorbet.

Nut butter is also great if you don't have a powerful blender that can chop hard nuts finely. However, a very powerful motor is required to turn cashew nuts into a tasty, smooth cream that can be frozen into nice cream. So these recipes are not just for those who own a powerful blender at home, but for anyone using a basic machine, too.

Try a variety of berries or super-powders for the base, and vary the sweetener—it's very easy to make your own nice cream. And feel free to enjoy it whenever—as a snack, for breakfast or as a scrumptious dessert!

Use different types of popsicle molds, or put the nice cream in a bowl and serve it immediately. You can top nice cream the same way you would bowls, and you can read more about this on p. 52.

STRAWBERRY NICE CREAM

MAKES 4 ICE CREAM POPSICLES

Nice cream can be made in several ways, the simplest being to just blend bananas and berries. For a fancier presentation, slice the fruit and berries, set them in the ice cream container, and cover the nice cream with a layer of chocolate.

BASIC RECIPE:

3 bananas

20–25 fresh strawberries, or defrosted if frozen

2 tbsp almond butter

optional, your choice of sweetener (4 dates, 1 tbsp honey or 1 tbsp maple syrup, for example)

In a food processor, blend the bananas and strawberries together with the almond butter. Add in your choice of sweetener, if desired. Freeze the mixture in popsicle molds for at least 6 hours.

VARIATIONS:

* Slice 4 strawberries, and add the slices to the side of the molds before you fill them with nice cream.
* Dip the frozen popsicles in chocolate sauce (see the recipe at right) and almond sprinkles (3 tablespoons of finely chopped almonds).

NICE CREAM CHOCOLATE SAUCE

This is the simplest of chocolate sauces, which can also double as a chocolate shell for nice cream popsicles. To liquefy the coconut oil, submerge the container in a bowl of warm tap water.

½ cup (1 dl) coconut oil

3 tbsp raw cacao powder

4 tbsp maple syrup or agave syrup

Make sure the coconut oil is liquid, and then stir in the remaining ingredients. Drizzle the chocolate sauce over the nice cream, or dip the popsicles in the sauce.

Psst! If you have some cacao butter at home, try using ½ cup of this instead of the coconut oil. If you can find cacao paste, you can skip half the coconut oil and all the cacao powder, and just add in the sweetener. Adding in different ingredients will modify the flavors.

COCONUT NICE CREAM
MAKES 4–6 POPSICLES

Try making chocolate nice cream by adding in raw cacao powder, or make half the nice cream plain and swirl the two creams beautifully inside the molds.

4 bananas
¾ cup (1½ dl) coconut cream
2 tbsp raw cacao nibs
1 tbsp raw cacao powder (optional)

Mix the bananas with the coconut cream in a blender. If you wish to add two colors to one mold, transfer half the ice cream to another bowl. Add cacao powder to the blender and mix. Stir cacao nibs into the ice cream in the bowl. Mix the two nice creams attractively in the molds and place the molds the freezer until the nice cream has set. This will take about 6 hours.

CRANBERRY ICE CREAM
MAKES 4–6 POPSICLES

Once, when I offered this nice cream to my family, they said, "This tastes just like store-bought!" I wondered if that was good or bad. But when my husband and children quickly tucked into their nice creams, I took that as a good sign.

Cranberries contribute a Nordic kind of acidity, in addition to good antioxidants. When you dip the popsicles in liquid cacao butter and coconut palm sugar, the combination of flavors is perfect.

5 tbsp cashew butter or almond butter
7 oz (200 g) frozen cranberries, defrosted
¼ cup (½ dl) maple syrup or 3 tbsp honey
TOPPING:
¼ cup (½ dl) cacao butter, melted
2 tbsp coconut palm sugar

In a blender, mix the cranberries and nut butter together with the maple syrup. Pour the mixture into molds and put them in the freezer for at least 6 hours. Melt the cacao butter in a warm water bath; stir in the coconut palm sugar. Remove the popsicles from the freezer and dip them quickly, one by one, in the cacao butter. Enjoy them immediately, or put them back in the freezer.

Juice Ices
Ices are super easy to make!
Put slices of fruit or berries
in ice cream molds, and fill
the molds with your favorite
juice.

COCONUT ICE

Coconut water is rehydrating and restores salt and mineral levels in the body, so it's perfect for hot summer days. It's even more refreshing when the coconut water is frozen into ices.

¼–½ cup (½–¾ dl) coconut water per popsicle mold

3 (frozen) raspberries and 2 small chunks of mango per popsicle mold

1 tsp coconut palm sugar per popsicle mold

Place the mango chunks and frozen raspberries in each mold, and fill the molds up with coconut water. Sprinkle with coconut palm sugar, and put the molds in the freezer for about 6 hours.

AVOCADO NICE CREAM
SERVES 4

Avocados, full of healthy fats, make the perfect base for nice cream. Their taste is pretty neutral, but their fat enhances the flavors of other ingredients. Black currants are acidic and characteristically Swedish, and have anti-inflammatory properties.

2 avocados

½ lb (225 gr) frozen black currants or cherries

2 tbsp yacon or maple syrup

TOPPING:

2 tbsp frozen or fresh black currants

2 tbsp bee pollen

yacon or maple syrup (optional)

In a blender, mix the avocado, frozen berries, and syrup to a smooth nice cream. Serve in bowls topped with frozen black currants and bee pollen, and some extra syrup if you want more sweetener.

HEARTY SNACKS

A small snack can also be filling. My snacks are often leftovers from lunch or dinner. So, try making those meals on the lighter side—and save what's left over for a snack. You'll put together these nibbles in less than 10 minutes. They're quick, they're tasty, and they are boosted with healthy nutrients!

Tips for snacks that can turn into lunch or dinner

A mylkshake and an energy bar • A green smoothie with a cinnamon ball • Zoodles with a raw brownie • Soup with chia crackers • Kale salad with a coconut ice for dessert • A bowl with a scrumptious topping • Chia pudding with dried fruit leather

KALE SALAD WITH CREAMY DRESSING
SERVES 3 TO 4

This creamy dressing can also double as a delicious dip for Friday evening cozy get-togethers. Change it up by adding in chopped black olives and sun-dried tomatoes, or capers and finely chopped green olives. Cut up some vegetable sticks, and you're ready to start dipping!

Here the boost comes from the white miso, which is umami—it has a sweet-and-sour flavor. Miso is made from soy, rice, salt, and water; this mix is left to ferment, assisted by koji fungus. Miso contains protein, and in traditional Chinese medicine it is thought to strengthen kidney function.

If your blender's motor is not powerful enough to handle nuts, replace the cashews with ½ cup (1 dl) of cashew butter.

7 kale or black cabbage leaves

DRESSING:

1 cup (2 dl) cashews

½ cup (1 dl) hemp hearts

1 tbsp apple cider vinegar

1 tbsp freshly squeezed lemon juice

A pinch of salt

1–1¾ cup (2–3½ dl) water

1 tbsp white miso

TOPPING:

3 tbsp sauerkraut

Seeds from ½ pomegranate

Rinse and strip the kale from the stem. Chop the kale into smaller pieces. Process the ingredients for the dressing in a blender. Start with a small amount of water and add a little bit by bit. Add and mix the dressing into the kale leaves, preferably using your hands. If you want to make a dip, process all the dressing's ingredients in a food processor instead. Top the salad with sauerkraut and pomegranate seeds.

2-MINUTE CARROT SOUP
SERVES 2

Speedy, raw, and tasty! For variety, replace the carrot juice with tomato or beet juice.

2 cups (5 dl) carrot juice
2 acovados, scooped
⅓" (1 cm) chili or dried chili
½" (1 cm) piece of fresh ginger
1–2 tsp tamari sauce (optional)

Process all the ingredients in a blender. Taste, and add more seasoning if needed.

CREAMY FENNEL SOUP
SERVES 2

Fresh fennel has a slight aniseed flavor; it has a cleansing effect and is good for the digestion. This almond mylk-based soup is inspired by a Spanish potage.

½ fennel bulb
¼ hothouse cucumber
1¾ cup (3 dl) almond mylk
Some freshly squeezed lemon juice
1 avocado, scooped
5–10 mint leaves (depending on strength of flavor; start off with 5)
5–10 lemon balm leaves
Herb salt
TOPPING:
3 tbsp chopped almonds
2 tbsp grated Parmesan cheese or nutritional yeast

Cut the fennel and cucumber into smaller chunks. Process them in a blender together with the other ingredients—except the topping—and season with more herb salt if needed. Top with Parmesan or—if you're a vegan—nutritional yeast.

SUPER CELERY SOUP
SERVES 2

Soup makes a great light supper or a hearty snack. For a day at the beach, bring this soup along in a thermos with ice cubes. Celery and cucumber regulate the body's balance of fluids and provides you with minerals that are beneficial for your skin.

4" (10 cm) hothouse cucumber
2 tomatoes
3 stalks celery
1 avocado
1 tbsp olive oil
A large pinch of dried Mediterranean oregano
A large pinch of dried basil
1–2 tsp herb salt
1 tbsp freshly squeezed lemon juice

Cut cucumber, tomatoes, and celery into chunks. Process them in a blender with the remaining ingredients, taste and adjust the soup for salt.

ZOODLES WITH BEST EVER TOMATO SAUCE
SERVES 2

Noodles without the carbohydrates are all the rage. Zucchini is a good alternative to regular noodles—preferably with a ridiculously tasty tomato sauce. You'll need a spiralizer to make the noodles, but you can make 'tagliatelle' strips just as effectively with a vegetable peeler. For a bit more "chew," layer the zucchini with carrot, parsnip, or daikon radish; it's nice also to mix zucchini noodles with kelp noodles. It's a great boost! Kelp noodles contain hardly any carbohydrates or calories but are rich in iodine, which is vital to our hormonal balance.

2 zucchini or 1 package kelp noodles
BEST EVER TOMATO SAUCE:
½ cup (¾ dl) sun-dried tomatoes
2 tomatoes
2 tsp balsamic vinegar
½–1 tbsp olive oil
A few pinches of rosemary
½ cup (1 dl) pumpkin seeds

Start by soaking the sun-dried tomatoes for 1 to 8 hours.
Turn the zucchini into noodles with a spiralizer, or make 'tagliatelle' using a vegetable peeler. If you're making kelp noodles, rinse them in a fine-meshed sieve, place them in a bowl, and cut them in half with a pair of scissors.
Cut the tomatoes into large chunks. Process them in a blender or food processor together with the remaining sauce ingredients, except for the pumpkin seeds. Add the seeds in and pulse them.
Fold the noodles into the sauce.

CHIA CRACKERS WITH TURMERIC GUACAMOLE

Once you've begun making your own almond mylk, you'll have quite a lot of almond pulp leftover, which makes an excellent base for balls or raw food crackers. They become like small cheese crackers—perfect for dipping!

You can easily save the almond pulp in a plastic bag and freeze it until you're ready to make the crackers, and why not make a double batch while you're at it? Nutritional yeast provides a tremendous boost with lots of vitamin B; it's also rich in protein. For vegans, nutritional yeast adds the flavor of cheese.

5 tbsp chia seeds
10 tbsp water
1½ cup (3 dl) almond pulp
½ cup (1 dl) nutritional yeast
2 pinches of salt
TURMERIC GUACAMOLE:
3 avocados
1 tomato
1 small red onion
A pinch of salt
1 tsp turmeric
A pinch of chili powder or chili flakes

Soak the chia seeds in 10 tablespoons of water for about one hour. In a bowl, mix together the chia seeds, almond pulp, nutritional yeast, and salt. Spread the mixture very thinly over a sheet of parchment paper. With the back of a knife, mark out 2" x 2" squares, which you divide diagonally. Dehydrate the crackers at 107°F (42°C) for about 20 hours, or until the crackers are thoroughly dried out. Store the crackers in a tin with a tight-fitting lid.

GUACAMOLE: In a bowl, mash the avocados with a fork (or mix them in a food processor) until you have a smooth cream. Dice the tomato and chop the onion, then mix them with the avocado. Add salt, turmeric, and chili. Taste and adjust for more salt or heat.

ZOODLES WITH AVOCADO PESTO
SERVES 2

Enjoy this dish for lunch, and save the leftovers for a snack. It will taste even better if it can sit for a while and let the zucchini strands soften a little.

Why not try the dressing on page 107 with these zoodles? The flavor is magical when you top them with a little nutritional yeast!

2 zucchinis or daikon radishes
AVOCADO PESTO:
½ cup (1 dl) pumpkin seeds
1 avocado
⅕ tsp garlic powder
½ container fresh basil
A pinch of salt
½–1 tbsp fresh lemon juice
1 tbsp olive oil
Freshly ground black pepper

Use a vegetable spiralizer to turn the zucchinis or radishes into noodles, or make tagliatelle using a root vegetable peeler.

AVOCADO PESTO: Grind the pumpkin seeds in a food processor. Add in the avocado, garlic powder, basil, and salt, then run the processor some more. While the machine is on, add in the lemon juice and olive oil, and blend until you have a smooth mixture. Season with more garlic, salt, or lemon juice, as needed. Finish it off with some freshly ground black pepper.

LUKEWARM AVOCADO SOUP WITH MISO

SERVES 2

The word 'soup' conjures up something that is hot, and yet we usually don't eat soup until it's lukewarm. Here you don't have to wait for the soup to cool down—it's at the right temperature right from the start. If you'd like a more substantial meal, boost the soup with cooked or sprouted quinoa, which provides extra protein and carbohydrates. Garlic suppresses viruses and gives your immune system extra strength during flu season.

5 sun-dried tomatoes

1¼ cup (2½ dl) warm water

2 tbsp dark miso paste

1 avocado

1 clove garlic or scant ¼ tsp garlic powder

TOPPING:

1 bunch of cilantro

2 lime wedges

Soak the tomatoes for 1 to 12 hours. Stir the miso into the warm water to dissolve it. Process the miso water together with the remaining ingredients—except the cilantro and lime—in a blender. Serve in bowls, and top each one with chopped fresh cilantro and a wedge of lime.

BALLS AND BARS

Tasty and healthy snacks, perfect to have on hand in the refrigerator and freezer

Balls and bars are a must for my refrigerator and freezer. They make my life so much easier! They're always close at hand when someone wants a bite to eat immediately, needs a snack to take with them, or when a craving for something sweet hits after a meal. The balls and bars are often made from what's already at home in the pantry, but here you'll find recipes and tips to get your own creative juices flowing.

My balls and bars are packed with good-for-you fats and crackling with antioxidants and protein—perfect snacks for both the young and the old!

Dehydration is a method of preserving food that has been around for hundreds of years. In raw food communities, a special drying oven—a dehydrator—is used. It can be set at 107°F (42°C) and has separate screens with netting and waxed parchment paper, all of which facilitate the dehydration process. But you can just as easily use a regular oven for drying food: Set it on its lowest temperature, right below 122°F (50°C), and use a wooden spoon to keep the door open just a crack if the oven doesn't have a convection setting. Drying times can vary a little depending on the oven you have, so be especially watchful when you first start drying food, and adjust the timing accordingly. The shelf life of dehydrated food will depend on how thoroughly it was dried.

I often snack on dehydrated food when I travel, since it stays fresh even when I don't have access to a refrigerator. Here's a tip, since you're doing this anyway: dehydrate food in larger batches, and stock up your snack pantry.

LICORICE LEATHER

MAKES 2 SHEETS

Licorice—it's almost impossible to resist! You can check on and adjust the licorice flavor by sampling it as you go along, but keep in mind that the flavor 'settles' during the dehydration process. Also, different licorice powders have different strengths. You can swap out the licorice powder for raw cacao powder or berry powder to vary the flavor of your leathers—but omit the salt flakes if you do.

6 bananas
3–4 tsp licorice powder
2 tbsp chia seeds
two pinches of salt flakes

In a blender, mix all ingredients except the salt flakes. Taste-test, and add more licorice powder if needed.

With a frying spatula, spread the mixture thinly over a sheet of waxed parchment paper; sprinkle with the salt flakes. Let the mixture dry on your oven's lowest temperature setting, about 107°F (42°C), for about 15 hours, or until all the mixture has dried out.

The mixture will dry a little more slowly in the middle, but you shouldn't dry it for too long or the leather will become brittle. The leather is meant to be slightly chewy. Cut the leather into strips and roll them up; store them in an airtight jar.

PRUNE AND BLUEBERRY LEATHER

MAKES 3 SHEETS

If you don't want to make strips, it can also be nice to use, say, gingerbread men molds to make little figures. Children love this—grown-ups, too. Prunes are very rich in vitamin A and K. And of course, a few prunes a day is excellent for intestinal health.

25 prunes
9 oz (250 g) frozen blueberries, defrosted

Soak the prunes for about 8 hours. Mix the prunes and the blueberries in a food processor to make a fruit batter.

Spread the batter onto waxed parchment paper, or pour a thin layer in molds. Let dry for about 15 hours. The leathers should be a bit chewy; cut them into strips and roll them up. Keep the leathers in an airtight jar.

Teenagers need lots of nourishment; a lot is going on in the body and loads of hormones are coursing around. As a result, it's very easy to turn to sugar and other fast-acting carbohydrates. But simple, filling, and naturally sweetened snacks provide the body with good quality calories, so stock the freezer with balls and bars and the refrigerator with chia puddings and overnight oats, and make sure your teen eats plenty of fruit and vegetables.

CRUNCHY RASPBERRY & COCONUT COOKIES
MAKES ABOUT 20 COOKIES

Oh boy—these small crunchy cookies are so good! I suggest making lots of them and sharing them with family and friends, or passing them around during the coffee break at work. They'll all be gone in the blink of an eye!

Lucuma powder adds sweetness, and helps bind the cookie dough together. Baobab powder also has a binding quality but has more of a tangy flavor and lots of vitamin C.

8 oz (225 g) frozen raspberries, defrosted—do not use the liquid

2¾ oz (75 g)—approx. 1¼ cup (2½ dl) coconut chips

1 tbsp baobab or lucuma powder

scant ¼ tsp vanilla powder

¼ cup (½ dl) coconut palm sugar

Stir together all the ingredients, but make sure to not include the liquid from the defrosted raspberries (save that juice in a glass and drink it!). Dot tablespoons of the mixture on waxed parchment paper and let the cookies dehydrate at 107°F (42°C) for about 20 hours. Store the cookies in an airtight jar.

FLAXSEED CRACKERS
MAKES 2 SHEETS

A sandwich for a snack? Sure! Layer avocado and tomato, put sunflower sprouts on top, or spread coconut oil instead of butter and top with sprouts and herb salt. It's a winning combo! Flaxseeds are rich in omega-3s, and wakame seaweed isn't merely salty and tasty, it's also loaded with minerals.

If you'd like to try to make sweet crackers, replace the stock and wakame in the batter with 2 tablespoons of honey and maybe some cinnamon.

½ cup (1 dl) golden flaxseeds

½ cup (1 dl) brown flaxseeds

½ cup (1 dl) chia seeds

5 cup (6 dl) water

½ cup (1 dl) hulled sesame seeds, with hulls

½ cup (1 dl) pumpkin seeds

½ tbsp stock powder

½ cup (1 dl) wakame seaweed

Soak the flaxseeds and chia seeds in 2½ cups (6 dl) of water for about 8 hours. Soak the sesame seeds and pumpkin seeds in a separate bowl with the remaining water for about 8 hours. Drain the water and mix the flaxseeds and chia seeds with the sesame and pumpkin seeds. Stir in the stock powder.

Cut the wakame seaweed into smaller bits and add them to the seed mixture. Spread the mixture thinly and evenly on a sheet of parchment paper or Teflex. Mark out squares with the back of a knife.

If you're making the crackers in a dehydrator, let them dry for about 5 hours at 107°F (42°C). Then take an empty tray and turn the crackers upside down onto the 'squared' side. Remove the parchment paper carefully and let the crackers dry for another 5 to 10 hours.

If you're using a conventional oven, turn the crackers over when you can loosen them from the parchment paper, and continue to dry the crackers until they are dry straight through. Break the crackers into the desired size.

CHIA SEED JAM

It's always good to have some chia jam in the refrigerator. You can use your choice of frozen or fresh berries or other fruits, and the jam will keep for about one week in the refrigerator. Enjoy the jam with pancakes, waffles, yogurt, or as topping for a bowl.

½ lb (225 gr) frozen or fresh berries or other fruit
5 apricots or dates
½ tbsp chia seeds
splash of freshly squeezed lemon juice

If you're using apricots, you'll need to soak the fruit first; if you're using dates, remove the pits. Process all the ingredients in a blender or food processor; transfer the jam to a jar and store in the refrigerator.

LICORICE PROTEIN BAR

Lemon and licorice is a winning combination! A delicious bar can be a reward after an exercise session, or be an energy booster before training. Here you'll find all the necessary amino acids and good fats that will help your muscles grow.

My advice is to make a large batch—they'll be gone far more quickly than you think.

½ cup (1 dl) black sesame seeds
1 cup (2 dl) pumpkin seeds
1 cup (2 dl) hemp protein powder
15 dates
3 tsp licorice powder
A large pinch of salt
3 tbsp freshly squeezed lemon juice

Mix sesame and pumpkin seeds in a food processor. Add the remaining ingredients and process until everything is thoroughly mixed. Spread the mixture on a sheet of parchment paper and shape the mixture into a rectangle using another piece of parchment paper placed on top. The rectangle should be ⅓" to ¾" thick (1 to 2 cm), and measure about 4"x 8" (10 cm x 20 cm). Cut it into bars of desired size. Lay some parchment paper between the bars, as if you were wrapping a sandwich.
These bars will keep for 1 to 2 weeks in the refrigerator, and for several months in the freezer.

SUPERFOOD CHOCOLATE CAKE

MAKES 1 LARGE CAKE OR 15 INDIVIDUAL PIECES

So, who doesn't enjoy a piece of dark chocolate in the afternoon? Or after lunch, or, well, at any time of the day? You can turn your square of chocolate into a super boost by adding in superfoods to it. It becomes total deliciousness that provides you with good fats, wholesome sweetness, and boosting powders rich in antioxidants.

¾ cup (1½ dl) or 3¼ oz (90 g) cacao butter

½ cup (1 dl) Brazil nuts

¼ cup (½ dl) hemp hearts

½ cup (1 dl) dried mulberries

pinch of salt

2 tbsp raw cacao powder

1 tbsp blueberry powder

¼ cup (½ dl) coconut palm sugar

tiny pinch of licorice powder

Break the cacao butter into smaller chunks and melt it over a lukewarm water bath. Chop the Brazil nuts coarsely. Place all the ingredients (except the cacao butter) in a bowl and mix well. Stir in the liquid cacao butter. Pour the mixture into a small baking pan lined with parchment paper or into muffin cups, and let the mixture set.

SUPERFOOD TRUFFLES

MAKES 15 TRUFFLES

Do you have three minutes to spare? Do you crave something sweet but still want to provide your body with the very best? Superfood truffles are a daily luxury; in our home they are often the delicious ending to a meal midweek. You can combine half amounts of tahini and almond butter, if you wish.

1½ cup (3 dl) tahini, or other type of nut or seed butter
¼ cup (½ dl) honey
1 tbsp lucuma powder
1 tbsp maca powder
2 tbsp raw carob powder
1 tbsp raw cacao powder
pinch of salt

In a bowl, stir together all the ingredients. Shape the mixture into small, pointy truffles; if it crumbles a bit, add in some more honey. Or if you're in a hurry, eat the mixture directly with a spoon. You can roll the truffles in extra cacao powder.

CHOCOLATE PUFFS

MAKES 6 MUFFIN CUPS

Quinoa is rich in protein, and quinoa puffs are scrumptious when mixed into balls and chocolate. The puffs are not categorized as raw food, but they're still a superfood! Use paper or silicone muffin cups, or try silicone ice cream molds.

The lucuma powder adds a gentle sweetness, a bit of creaminess, and of course lots of goodness in the form of antioxidants, calcium, and iron.

½ cup (1 dl) cacao butter
¼ cup (½ dl) coconut oil
1½ cup (3 dl) quinoa puffs
2 tbsp raw cacao powder
¼ cup (½ dl) agave, maple, or yacon syrup
1 tbsp lucuma powder (optional)

Melt the cacao butter and coconut oil over a lukewarm water bath. Stir in the quinoa puffs, cacao powder, syrup, and lucuma powder. With a spoon, fill the muffin cups halfway. Store in the freezer. These taste best eaten while still chilled, since the cocoa butter and coconut oil will melt after a while.

Pure Dark Chocolate

If you want pure dark chocolate without anything in it, omit the puffs, and pour the mixture into ice-cube trays.

CHERRY BARS
MAKES ABOUT 12 BARS

Protein bars provide a boost when you're in training—you can easily make them at home and load up quickly as needed for your activity. Protein bars often taste more 'good-for-you' than a yummy ball, but your homemade bars are free of added white sugar and preservatives, and they'll provide you with all necessary amino acids.

heaped ½ cup (1½ dl) + ¼ cup (½ dl) pumpkin seeds

½ cup (1 dl) almonds

10 dates

Grated zest from one lemon

½ lb (225 g) frozen cherries, defrosted

½ cup (1 dl) hemp powder

½ cup (½ dl) chia seeds

Chop all the pumpkin seeds in a food processor. Remove them and transfer ¼ cup (½ dl) of the chopped pumpkin seeds to a bowl. Put the almonds in the food processor and grind them together with the pumpkin seeds until they are mixed into flour.

Remove the pits from the dates, and add the dates, grated lemon zest, cherries (reserving their liquid), hemp powder, and chia seeds to the food processor and mix everything into a batter, diluting it if necessary with some cherry juice. The mixture shouldn't be completely dry, but not too sticky either.

Shape the mixture into a rectangle measuring about 4" x 8" (10 x 20 cm) on a sheet of parchment paper. Dip the rectangle into the saved pumpkin mix so you have mixed seeds on both sides. Cut into approximately 12 pieces. Store the bars wrapped in parchment paper, in the freezer.

Remove the bars from the freezer when you're ready to eat them. They will defrost in no time and have the perfect texture.

CINNAMON BALLS
MAKES ABOUT 10 BALLS

The cinnamon bun is, after all, a classic coffee break treat, isn't it? Personally, I just want the yummy inside of the bun, which is why I love this version.

DOUGH:

1 cup (2 dl) almonds, soaked or dry

½ cup (1 dl) sulfate-free raisins

1 tbsp coconut oil, softened (but not liquid)

1 tsp ground cinnamon

½ tsp ground cardamom

½ tsp vanilla powder

A pinch of salt

FILLING:

10 dates

1 tbsp coconut oil, softened (but not liquid)

3–4 tsp ground cinnamon

½ tbsp water

Grind the almonds in a food processor until they are finely chopped. Add the remaining ingredients for the dough and process until everything is mixed. Shape the dough into balls.

Would you like to make something more sophisticated? Roll out the dough between two sheets of parchment paper to make a rectangle measuring about 4" x 8" (10 x 20 cm). Remove the pits from the dates that will make the filling. Mix the dates and coconut oil, cinnamon, and ½ tbsp water in the food processor. Spread the filling over the rectangle, leaving a border of about ¾" (2 cm) along the long sides. Use the parchment paper to help you roll up the rectangle. Put the roll in the refrigerator or in the freezer.

The roll will be softer if stored in the refrigerator and it will keep for about one week. The dough will harden in the freezer but the filling will remain soft. The roll will keep for several months in the freezer. You can also try drying it in the dehydrator for about 20 hours at 107°F–113°F (42°C–45°C). If you do this, slice the roll into pieces and transfer them into bun molds.

RAW CRUMBLE
MAKES 1 SMALL PIE

A perfect, delicious, and awesomely good-for-you snack!

½ cup (1 dl) almonds

8 dates

½ cup (1 dl) grated coconut

1 cup (2 dl) rolled oats

1 tsp salt

1 tbsp coconut oil, softened

SUGGESTIONS FOR 3 DIFFERENT FILLINGS:

1¼–1¾ cup (3–4 dl) fresh berries

½ lb (225 gr) frozen berries, defrosted

4 apples, chopped in the food processor with 8 soaked (dried) apricots

Run the almonds in a food processor until they are finely chopped. Remove the pits from the dates. Add the remaining ingredients, except the filling, and process until everything is mixed to make a dough. Set ¼ of the dough aside to make a crumble to sprinkle over the filling, and press out the remaining dough into a pie pan measuring about 8" (20 cm) in diameter. Fill the pie shell with any of the suggested fillings and sprinkle crumbs of the set aside dough over the top.

For a warm version of this pie, place the pie in a dehydrator or conventional oven at 107°F (42°C) for 4 to 8 hours.

By all means, serve this pie with some cashew cream made from cashew nuts, water, and honey.

DELECTABLE MANGO BALL WITH LICORICE
MAKES 10 BALLS

There's room for many flavor nuances in this ball— mango meets ginger, which gets a hint of coconut and a touch of salty licorice. Many different healthy ingredients get paired up, too: Mango contributes vitamins A and C; ginger gets the digestion running smoothly; the good fats from coconut and cashews ensure that you have a complete snack.

1 cup (2 dl) dried mango, soaked

2¼ cup (5 dl) cashews

1¼" (3 cm) piece of fresh ginger

A pinch of salt

GARNISH:

½ cup (1 dl) grated coconut

2 tsp licorice powder

Soak the dried mango for 4 to 8 hours. Grind the cashews in a food processor; add in the mango slices. Reserve the soaking water if you need to dilute the mix (otherwise you can use it as a liquid base for a smoothie).

Add the ginger and the salt, and process until you have a dough that's sturdy enough to roll into balls.

Mix the grated coconut and the licorice powder in a bowl. Roll the balls in the coconut mix. Store the balls in the refrigerator.

COFFEE SQUARES
MAKES 10 SQUARES

Calling all coffee lovers! This is the square (or ball—whichever you like) for you. I'm not a coffee drinker but I won't say no thanks to a hint of coffee flavor. You can choose your preferred flavor strength by adding more or less coffee granules. As you know, coffee will perk you up because it contains caffeine, but the coffee bean also contains antioxidants. You can also use decaffeinated coffee.

2¼ cup (5 dl) cashews
10 dates
1–2 tbsp instant coffee granules (decaffeinated works, too)
1–2 tbsp water
½ tsp vanilla powder
2 tsp reishi powder (optional)

Chop the cashews in a food processor until they are finely ground. Remove the pits from the dates and add to the cashews. Add in 1 tablespoon coffee granules, 1 table-spoon water, and then the remaining ingredients. Taste, and add more coffee granules and water if needed. Shape into small squares measuring about 1¼ x 1¼" (3 x 3 cm).

REISHI
Reishi has been used in traditional Chinese medicine for over 2,000 years. This medicinal fungus is dried and pulverized, and then added to beverages (tonics), chocolate, or to different culinary dishes. Reishi creates energy, calm, and strength, and boosts our immune system. It can also have an effect on sleep, and helps us handle everyday stress.

THE SIMPLEST RAW BROWNIE
MAKES ABOUT 10 BROWNIES

Once you've tried this recipe, you'll wonder how something so simple can taste so good! This raw brownie easily beats regular brownies, both in wholesomeness and in flavor.

1 cup (2 dl) + ½ cup (1 dl) walnuts
10 dates
3 tbsp raw cacao powder
pinch of salt

Pulverize 1 cup (2 dl) walnuts in the food processor. Remove the pits from the dates. Add in the dates, cacao powder and salt, and process until you have a dough. Stir in the remaining walnuts. Press the dough into a small mold, or shape it into a square and cut into smaller squares. Store in the refrigerator.

RAW BROWNIE DELUXE
• Place the dough into a mold, and pour chocolate sauce over the dough (see p. 99). Chill it in the refrigerator until the sauce has set.
• If you'd like to make Love Treats, omit the extra walnuts and add 1 teaspoon of vanilla powder and 1 tablespoon of coconut oil instead. Press out the dough into a small mold, pour the chocolate sauce over it, and sprinkle with coconut flakes. Chill it in the refrigerator until the chocolate has set.
• To make a minty brownie, add 2 tablespoons of peppermint honey (see p. 95).
A basic recipe with many possible variations!

CHIA BARS WITH MATCHA TEA AND DRIED GROUND-CHERRIES

MAKES ABOUT 12 BARS

If you go straight from work to your exercise session, you are likely to need a boost! Matcha tea and maca powder both provide you with extra energy. This bar has all the essential amino acids; the ground-cherries are loaded with vitamin C, and they also contain plenty of protein!

2¼ cup (2½ dl) cashews
¼ cup (½ dl) chia seeds
2 tsp matcha powder
½ tbsp maca powder
2 tsp freshly squeezed lemon juice
1 tbsp water
pinch of salt
12–14 soft figs (if not soft, soak them for a while)
½ cup (1 dl) ground-cherries

Mix the cashews with the chia seeds in a food processor. Add all the ingredients—except the ground-cherries—and process some more. Fold in the ground-cherries and shape into bars with the help of a sheet of parchment paper.

NUT-FREE CRANBERRY BALLS

MAKES ABOUT 10 BALLS

Dried cranberry powder is a concentrated form of cranberry; it's an awesome alternative to fresh berries because the wholesome cranberries become even better for you! These balls are also boosted with pumpkin seeds, a superb source for zinc that maintains our body's metabolism.

1¼ cup (2½ dl) pumpkin seeds
¾ cup (1½ dl) sunflower seeds
4 tbsp coconut oil, softened
¼ cup + 1 tsp honey (¾ dl)
2 tbsp cranberry powder
pinch of salt
some cranberry powder, for dusting (optional)

Mix the pumpkin and sunflower seeds in a food processor until they are finely ground. Add in the remaining ingredients and process until you can make balls out of the mixture. Try rolling the balls in cranberry powder.

EASY CHOCOLATE BALLS
MAKES ABOUT 10 BALLS

This is such a simple recipe that kids can make these balls by themselves. The recipe requires neither a food processor nor a blender—just a bowl and a big spoon. When my daughter Saga wants something sweet to snack on, she declares: "I'm going to make batter!" She then pulls a bit of this and a little of that out of the pantry, mixes up a batter and eats it by spoonful straight from the bowl. Oats are rich in good fats, which actually helps with weight loss.

½ cup (1 dl) nut butter
½ cup (1 dl) rolled oats
1 tbsp mylk, water, or cold coffee
2 tbsp raw cacao powder
3 tbsp honey
¼ cup (½ dl) grated coconut

Mix everything together in a bowl. Roll the batter into balls, and then roll the balls in grated coconut; or, eat the batter with a spoon directly from the bowl.

BLUEBERRY PIE BALLS
MAKES ABOUT 10 BALLS

A traditional blueberry pie is made with pie pastry and blueberries, and served with cream or vanilla custard. Here you get it all in one go, and all the essential nutrients are kept intact. Be careful when you share these blueberry balls—all of a sudden there may be none left for you …

You can prepare a mini blueberry pie by tripling the quantities and pressing it into a small spring-form pan. Put it in the refrigerator for about 6 hours, and garnish it with fresh or dried blueberries.

1¼ cup (3 dl) cashews
2 tsp blueberry powder
1–2 tbsp honey
1 tbsp coconut oil
½ tsp vanilla powder
pinch of salt
heaped ¼ cup (¾ dl) dried blueberries

Chop the cashews in a food processor until they are finely ground, add the remaining ingredients except the dried blueberries, and keep mixing until a dough forms. Fold in the dried blueberries. Roll out balls, or shape the dough into a circle and cut out small pie slices instead.

Kids are unequivocal about what they like and don't like, but they can also be curious about new flavors. It's good to avoid white sugar, which destabilizes blood sugar levels and mood, so try replacing regular chocolate milk with chocolate mylk, for example, or make nice cream together; why not make raw food balls, which they can shape themselves!

NUT BUTTER
MAKES 1 JAR

Homemade nut butter—it's simple and delicious, and you know it's made fresh. Nut butter is the perfect topping, whether on a sandwich or on slices of apple, hothouse cucumber or zucchini. It's also a scrumptious base for raw food balls. The neutral oil is flavorless, but if you like the taste of cold-pressed canola, that will work too.

White almond butter is made from blanched almonds—almonds that have been steamed to remove their skins. This gives them a milder taste and a totally white color. You can make your own white almond butter with skinless almonds, or buy white almond butter. You can even find different brands of raw, white almond butter.

1 cup, heaped (5 dl) nuts/seeds/almonds
¼ cup–¾ cup (½ dl–1½ dl) neutral-tasting oil
pinch of salt (optional)

Mix the nuts or seeds of your choice, or almonds, in a food processor, adding in the neutral oil and salt. Different nuts will call for different amounts of oil. Cashews only need about ¼ cup (½ dl) of oil, while almonds will need ¾ cup (1½ dl) to become a really creamy nut butter. Store the butter in a glass jar with a tight-fitting lid.

If you'd like to make coconut butter, simply grind a 7 oz. (200 g) bag of grated coconut in the food processor for about 10 to 15 minutes. To start the mixing process, add in a tablespoon of coconut oil.

Psst . . .
To make a quick nut mylk,
blend nut butter and water!

TRAIL MIX

There are times when there just isn't enough time to pull out the food processor or blender, and that's when a trail mix is perfect. The name stems from the portable medley that can be a real lifesaver on the trail. And even if we aren't traveling along a path in the wilderness but more along life's trail, this trail mix comes to the rescue when a quick snack is needed.

Here are my favorite four quick mixes, but do try mixes using what you already have in your pantry. Each mix has its own specific nutritional profile, but all are packed with antioxidants, good fats, and protein—perfect snacks!

- ½ cup (1 dl) cacao nibs, ½ cup (1 dl) goji berries, ¾ cup (1½ dl) pumpkin seeds
- ½ cup (1 dl) ground-cherries, 1 cup (2 dl) cashews, ½ cup (1 dl) cacao nibs
- ½ cup (1 dl) mulberries, ½ cup (1 dl) coarsely chopped almonds, ½ cup (1 dl) grated coconut
- ½ cup (1 dl) raisins, ½ cup (1 dl) hazelnuts (filberts), 3 tbsp whole cacao beans, ½ cup (1 dl) sunflower seeds

RECIPE INDEX

Thank You!

To all nutrients lying hidden in magical raw ingredients, which allows us humans to live life to the fullest. To my family, relatives, and friends, who encourage me in my creative endeavors with love and patience. To my publisher Cecilia Viklund, editor Åsa Karsberg, art director Kai Ristilä, and photographer Bianca Brandon-Cox for fantastic and creative teamwork. And, thank you to Elin Lannsjö, Västergården, Calle Forsberg, and Anna Lindell for the loan of such beautiful ceramics.

CONVERSION CHARTS
METRIC AND IMPERIAL CONVERSIONS
(These conversions are rounded for convenience)

Ingredient	Cups/Tablespoons/Teaspoons	Ounces	Grams/Milliliters
Butter	1 cup/16 tablespoons/2 sticks	8 ounces	230 grams
Cheese, shredded	1 cup	4 ounces	110 grams
Cream cheese	1 tablespoon	0.5 ounce	14.5 grams
Cornstarch	1 tablespoon	0.3 ounce	8 grams
Flour, all-purpose	1 cup/1 tablespoon	4.5 ounces/0.3 ounce	125 grams/8 grams
Flour, whole wheat	1 cup	4 ounces	120 grams
Fruit, dried	1 cup	4 ounces	120 grams
Fruits or veggies, chopped	1 cup	5 to 7 ounces	145 to 200 grams
Fruits or veggies, pureed	1 cup	8.5 ounces	245 grams
Honey, maple syrup, or corn syrup	1 tablespoon	0.75 ounce	20 grams
Liquids: cream, milk, water, or juice	1 cup	8 fluid ounces	240 milliliters
Oats	1 cup	5.5 ounces	150 grams
Salt	1 teaspoon	0.2 ounce	6 grams
Spices: cinnamon, cloves, ginger, or nutmeg (ground)	1 teaspoon	0.2 ounce	5 milliliters
Sugar, brown, firmly packed	1 cup	7 ounces	200 grams
Sugar, white	1 cup/1 tablespoon	7 ounces/0.5 ounce	200 grams/12.5 grams
Vanilla extract	1 teaspoon	0.2 ounce	4 grams

OVEN TEMPERATURES

Fahrenheit	Celsius	Gas Mark
225°	110°	¼
250°	120°	½
275°	140°	1
300°	150°	2
325°	160°	3
350°	180°	4
375°	190°	5
400°	200°	6
425°	220°	7
450°	230°	8